THE ORCHARD

DIAL PRESS
TRADE PAPERBACK

THE
ORCHARD

A Memoir

Adele Crockett Robertson

With a foreword and epilogue
by Betsy Robertson Cramer

THE ORCHARD

A Dial Press Trade Paperback / published by arrangement with Henry Holt and Company, Inc.

This edition contains the complete text of the original hardcover edition.
NOT ONE WORD HAS BEEN OMITTED.

PUBLISHING HISTORY
Metropolitan Books hardcover edition published 1995
Bantam trade paperback edition / February 1997
A Dial Press Trade Paperback / June 2005

Published by
The Dial Press
A Division of Random House, Inc.
New York, New York

ISBN 0-553-37859-7

The Dial Press and Dial Trade Paperbacks are registered trademarks of Random House, Inc.,
and the colophon is a trademark of Random House, Inc.

Printed in the United States of America
Published simultaneously in Canada

www.dialpress.com

10 9 8 7

FOREWORD

Among our most haunting images of the Great Depression is that of the man in the suit and hat selling apples on a city street, charging a nickel apiece. *The Orchard* is the story of where those apples came from, of the life that was lived on one farm during those difficult years, of the apple orchard that my mother kept from 1932 to 1934, just outside the small mill town of Ipswich, Massachusetts.

My mother's father had just died, his medical practice swamped by the unpaid bills of unemployed patients. Her mother and younger brothers were in Boston struggling to survive. The family farm was all but lost to the bank when my mother, with only her Great Dane, Freya, for company, gave up the safe, white-collar city job that her Radcliffe education had secured and returned to the farm, the orchard. "I determined," she wrote years later, "not to mourn, but to throw my lot in with the trees, certain that somehow they and we would survive. These fields and this old house in which we had all been born would never be lost. The apple orchard and the peach trees would save us all. I never doubted that this was my destiny. No one else shared my optimism, but . . . what else was there to do? I remember walking out among the trees, bare now and stark, but in my mind's eye I pictured them in blossom, in leaf, and at last loaded with fruit, the golden apples of the Hesperides."

Adele LeBourgeois Crockett Robertson—known to all as Kitty— was born in 1901 in the same Massachusetts seacoast town where, a little more than seventy-eight years later, she died. For my mother, Ipswich was always home. Her father, Dr. Eugene A. Crockett, had bought the former country boardinghouse with its dairy and hay farm in November 1897. To the west, a small canal, the Hay or Fox Creek Canal, cut across the salt marsh and connected the Castle Neck River to the Ipswich River, itself a pathway from the ocean to the town. To the east, more salt marsh bordered a magnificently wild barrier now known as Crane Beach.

The farm, an island of glacial till and clay rising from the surrounding salt marsh and creeks, was attached to the town of Ipswich by Argilla Road. At the turn of the century, wrote W. S. Shurcliff in a local history:

It was narrow, being only a little wider than a wagon; and, of course, it was a dirt road. . . . There were few trees along the road, and only a few bushes. The traveler had an almost unimpeded view of the bare drumlins, the flat salt marshes, and an occasional farm.

By the early 1930s, Ipswich's thirty-three square miles were home to a population of about six thousand. Except for the Argilla Road community of summer people—city people—it was a blue-collar town, quite unlike its more homogeneous and affluent North Shore neighbors. Years later, my mother proudly claimed to other Ipswich citizens that she, too, was a native, "born on the Argilla Road." "Hell," joked a town fellow, "that ain't Ipswich." True enough, few residents of "the road" had been known to share, or even to see, the difficult lives of their neighbors. Kitty was one of the exceptions.

The town had long been divided into separate neighborhoods, jobs, and ethnic groups. From the early part of the century, the Ipswich Mills, then the world's largest hosiery factory, was the town's chief employer. Staffed with mostly foreign workers, the Mills experienced no shortage of labor, despite bitter strikes. The workers formed their own distinct communities: the Poles in company-owned and -built housing adjacent to the mill, the Greeks a few blocks away, the French Canadians, Irish, and other immigrants scattered throughout the town.

By 1927, the tentacles of the coming Depression had reached Ipswich. The next year, the Ipswich Mills closed for good. Almost half of the wage earners in the town had been employed by the Mills. The rest were clammers, farmers, farm employees, or small businessmen. At one smaller hosiery mill, my mother would later apply for a job.

The annual Town Reports of Ipswich during that period tell a story that reflects the national crisis. Each year they grew gloomier. 1931: "The hardest year since the Depression began." 1932: "An immediate improvement in the labor situation is a forlorn hope. Finding jobs is out of the question. They cannot even be bought. Our clamming areas, from time immemorial the resort of those temporarily out of employment, always prolific hitherto, are now nearly depleted." 1933: Ipswich's "hardest year yet, banks failing, banks closed, business stagnant, and labor unemployed. It is no mean problem to ride out the storm."

The whole nation went hungry, and in its pastures of plenty the farmer slaved, starved, and was sold up. Cheaper to burn than to market, corn was shoveled into the furnaces of an Iowa courthouse. Surplus eggs and cream flooded rural ditches, potatoes froze in the ground, and crops dropped off the trees as the price of fruit fell below the cost of picking and packing. Frantic shippers offered apples on credit to the unemployed for $1.75 a crate, as President Herbert Hoover's economic prescription of private charity and individual self-reliance was embodied in Damon Runyon's Apple Annie. By the end of November 1930, notes historian T. H. Watkins, "there were six thousand apple sellers on the streets of New York City alone, crouching, in the words of newspaperman Gene Fowler, 'like half-remembered sins sitting upon the conscience of the town.'" At every corner a figure of dignity and despair loomed behind an upturned crate.

Burdened by falling prices, taxes, and debt, 750,000 farmers forfeited their homesteads in forced sales between 1930 and 1935. Farmers everywhere were desperate. It was in these circumstances that my mother returned to Ipswich to save the orchard. "It was a time to try the soul," she wrote later. "There was the beginning of the long slide into despair, the breadlines, the apple sellers shivering on street corners, the runs on the bank, factories and businesses closing down. Proud people went shamefaced to the 'Gimme Store' and came away with whatever was surplus that week. There were occasions when, dead tired and discouraged, I wondered whether apples alone would keep our sinking ship afloat."

By 1934, the New Deal's Economic Recovery had stepped in to help find work for breadwinners on welfare. Even so, the Ipswich Town Report for 1935 tells of the "utter impossibility of obtaining employment." The outlook for 1936 was hardly more promising: "Things may be better, but Ipswich hasn't much to offer to better things with."

So it continued down to wartime, when a shipyard built alongside Fox Creek provided jobs for six hundred men and one woman: my mother. Then Sylvania moved some of its assembly lines into the old mill buildings, employing more than five hundred workers; eventually, she became one of them. Boston, reborn, required suburbs. Slowly, Ipswich came back to life.

THOSE terrible Depression years are the backdrop to *The Orchard*, the story of one woman, struggling at the end of a country road to make a living from a little apple orchard, and enduring with the help of others who were even worse off. There were no trumpets, no medals, but the heroism was real: to work was to fight. When President Franklin Delano Roosevelt told the nation that "the only thing we have to fear is fear itself," she was sitting by the radio, "all alone in the cold house, hungry, discouraged, with a cellarful of unsold apples that was to keep the wolf from the door," and felt a "thrill of hope . . . a sense of inevitable victory."

Twenty years later—when much was won, but much also, for her, was lost—there was a lull in my mother's life. Although I was too young to know why she decided to write or to appreciate what she was writing, I remember clearly her intensity, the daily hours at the typewriter. But fewer than twelve months passed before her life again became a hurricane. She was unable to finish her book.

Cleaning up after my mother's death, I found these pages at the bottom of a bookcase, under old telephone books and stacks of paper. They traveled unread around the country with me until two winters ago when—housebound in Ipswich—I returned with my mother to that colder and harder time.

Today's visitors to Crane Beach pass by the remnants of the orchard. The road has been widened, and on hot summer weekends it is jammed in both directions. Three quarters of a mile from the thronged beach sits the old farmhouse, now very close to the road, its protecting elms gone, one downed by a hurricane, its mate strangled by Dutch elm disease. To the left, if you look, a few scrawny, sparse-leafed fruit trees stand on the hillside. Elaborate houses or weeds have sprung where once were peaches and apples.

Here and there, an old tree still yields its wormy and abandoned crops. For me, the pages that follow have given each leaf, each apple, a kind of voice. They whisper of a time of challenge, struggle, success, and of the young Kitty Crockett, my mother, in her years of bitter glory.

—*Betsy Robertson Cramer*

THANKS

It is a pleasure to acknowledge those who have helped me bring my mother's manuscript to publication. Among those who have shared their ideas with me are my friends Jan David, Daniel Corrigan, Judy Raymond, Sharon Josephson, Mary Lela Sherburne, Barbara K. Baring-Gould, the late Edward D. Baring-Gould, and my cousin Susan Glessner. I am especially grateful to Nancy Thompson and Oliver Coolidge. My thanks go as well to literary agent Nina Ryan for her invaluable enthusiasm and skill. They all helped bring *The Orchard* alive, and I know my mother would be pleased with what has become a shared effort. Two of my mother's friends, Ipswich historian Mary Patch Conley and Elizabeth Vincent Foster, also encouraged me. I think that Kitty would have been proud to dedicate this, her book, to both Elizabeth and Mary, with love.

—*BRC*

THE ORCHARD

My father died in the spring of 1932, suddenly, quietly, in his sleep. I was the one who found him. I went to tell him that breakfast was ready, and even though I had never seen a dead person before, I knew that he was gone. His glasses were on the table within reach, his watch undisturbed beside the pillow. As I stood looking down at him I thought that if he had felt the approach of death he would have moved to put his glasses on—his first gesture always, as he was almost blind without them. He had not moved: he had not known, and that seemed strange to me.

Yet in a way he must have felt a foreboding like the one that had gripped me when I went to call him. For once, he was not downstairs ahead of us all, laughing and kidding with Jessie, the cook, in the kitchen that smelled richly of coffee and bacon. Only the night before we had sat talking after everyone had gone to bed. The house was very still. The clock ticked in the hall, and Freya, the Great Dane, stirred and snuffled on her rug, but outside the elm branches were quiet and there was not even a whisper from the sea. He spoke of the farm and of the first time he had seen it, as a boy of eight, almost sixty years before.

He recalled the long train ride from Maine to Boston for a seven-day visit with his uncle and aunt from Somerville, who had rented a cottage by the sea for a week. He had been invited as companion to his cousin, Will, also an only child. For seven days the boys ran free: fished for minnows, sailed toy boats in the salt creeks, and, adventuring across a half mile of marshes, first set foot on the newly mown stubble of the north hayfield of the farm.

"I have been thinking all day about the week we spent in that cottage at the foot of Sagamore Hill," he said. "It's funny, but I haven't remembered it for years. And then today I could almost feel again the prick of the stubble on my bare feet when Will and I crossed the marsh, ploughed through the mud of Fox Creek at low tide, and scrambled over the stone wall and into the hayfield. We were jumping in the haycocks when the hired man came down and told us that we had better get out of there. He said the horses wouldn't eat the hay after we had played in it and that they would still be able to smell us way next winter. Cows, he said, weren't so fussy. He was a nice sort of man, because as we were walking away he called to us and said we could play in the big stack of marsh hay on the staddle, the cluster of stakes to keep the hay above the tide. The horses wouldn't eat that anyway, he said, because it was salty."

From the top of the big haystack, warm and salt-smelling in the sun, the boys looked out over the acres of the farm, the ridged terminal moraine of the glacier that lay curled like a sleeping dog on the green rug of the marsh.

"That day," said my father, "I told Will that I was coming back here sometime and was going to buy that farm and have it for my own.

"I did not see it again for twenty years," he continued, "but I thought of it all the way home to Maine and often afterward until hard times in the family gave me other things to think about."

On that last evening, when he got up to put the screen in front of the fire and slide the shutters across the small-paned windows, he recalled how, after his father had died and he had struggled his way through medical school, he had been invited to spend a few days in Ipswich by another young doctor. He had known only that they were going duck hunting, and it was not till they were three miles out of town and the salt marshes began to unroll on either side of the causeway that he suddenly realized where he was.

"I saw the cottage at Sagamore still standing after all those years," he said, "and then I knew for sure. The farm would be mine." Two years later he went back and purchased the farm with the first money he earned.

Old trees shaded the farmhouse. In front rose the immense elm, planted in 1760 when the house was built, the huge trunk rising twenty feet before dividing into three main branches, each supporting a fountain of leaves and twigs. I never could climb the tree or even reach the first fork with its saddle of green moss. The orioles swung their hammocks in the elm every spring. Their bubbling, flute-like song swelled the morning chorus of the birds; their flame-and-black bodies flashed among the leaves.

To the west stood the linden that was the family pride. My father used to say that the glorious green cone sheltering the weathered clapboards of the old square house clinched his decision to buy the farm. The vast trunk was groined like the arches of a cathedral; the branches were muscled like a giant's arm. It was an English linden with small leaves, round and dark. Always, around the Fourth of July, the entire tree blossomed, even to the topmost branch: pale, waxy blossoms so sweet that the humans who dwelt in its shade were bemused like the bees that rumbled and tumbled among the flowers.

Between the linden and the big elm, a smaller elm—his wife, my grandmother said—struggled for existence. Fed, pruned, and cherished, still the wife always looked peaked. A tree doctor who came to treat her told my father that a root of one of the larger trees was strangling her deep under the ground. "There is as much below the ground as above it," he said to my father; "for every leaf and twig there is a corresponding rootlet." In my mind's eye, I saw a whole tree of roots underground, like a reflection in a pond, with a Laocoön's serpent coiling around the poor wife and slowly throttling her to death.

When my father first acquired the farm there was also an orchard of about fifty apple trees—Baldwins, Northern Spies, Russets, and old varieties now forgotten: Blue Pearmains, Winter Bananas, and a Porter apple tree near the kitchen door from which my grandmother made a rich, dark, golden jelly every year. Back then, there was something left of the pioneer's effort to prepare for the arduous, cold months ahead when the ground was iron hard and no longer produced food for the family. There were the apples to pick and sort over into barrels and to be stored in the cellar. The Rhode Island Greenings came from the tree with the short, thick trunk and the low branches almost sweeping the ground; these were the pie apples with rich granular juicy flesh—good through Thanksgiving. There were the

Baldwins, red and firm, and the crimson-streaked Northern Spies that lasted into January. Last were the Russets, wrinkled but still quite tasty into April. There were potatoes to dig and trundle down to the cellar. The last of the tomatoes were brought into the house to ripen in a sunny window, and the grapes were stripped from the old vine whose trunk was as thick as a child's leg.

The apple harvest was the great event of my childhood: everyone gay and laughing, the piles of red-cheeked apples in the fine frosty grass, the smell of wood smoke in the air. The trees planted before the Revolutionary War were so high that it took an extension ladder to reach the tops. It was my father's job, assisted sometimes by neighborhood men and boys, to climb the ladder with a bushel basket that hung from an S-hook from the highest rungs and to pick the reddest apples from branches bathed in sunlight all summer long. With a smaller basket, hanging from a cord around my neck, I scrambled among the high branches, gathering the apples that the ladder would not reach, running along the tree limbs like a squirrel. I knew every hand- and foothold from a summer of climbing. Autumn gales and winter ice storms felled those old trees, one by one, till all were gone.

MY GRANDMOTHER had always managed the practical aspects of the farm, tending the cows and the chickens, efficiently overseeing every detail of the work. Much of it she did herself. After she died my father learned the high cost of hiring workers to do what she had done from love. Without my grandmother's attentions, the cows sickened and the chickens died. Eventually my father—living with our family in Boston and busy with his medical practice—saw that it wasn't possible to run a farm only on weekends, but still he wouldn't give up altogether. Fruit, that was the thing. You planted trees and they grew. When you were ready for them, there they were. There is a wonderful continuity about fruit trees.

And so, in the springs following World War I, the cornfields and the hay meadows were set out to apples, while the black earth of the Indian midden where my grandmother's vegetable garden had flourished among the rotting clam shells of old summer feasts was planted to peaches. As my father and I set the smooth-barked whips into the lines of holes, he wondered who would harvest the fruit from these trees in a hundred years. A great deal was expected from those trees by the two optimists who planted them. Year after year, they would go on thrusting their roots down into the glacial soil of the hillside, their branches high and wide against the grassy slope. After blossoming gloriously, all pink and white in the spring, there would be barrels and boxes of perfect fruit in the fall.

"They will take care of me in my retirement," my father said with satisfaction, looking down at the neat rows of frail little sticks from which so much was hoped and promised.

All through the years when I was frolicking about from job to job, the trees were growing. Occasionally I could take a vacation and come home during the harvest. It did not seem very businesslike, but it was fun. Neighbors, friends, schoolchildren, and passersby picked the apples. Everyone got paid and had a great time. There was time out for tea, time out for ice cream, time out for apple fights among the kids. There was a fine big tractor in the barn where the horse stalls had been and an expensive fruit grader in the calf pen. The haymows were piled to the roof with boxes and shooks. There were parts of beehives and a honey extractor in a corner. It was a big industry, and the fruit was beautiful. The cement storage cellar under the barn could hold all of a bumper crop, and bumper crops were going to be the rule in this orchard.

My father's health began to fail in 1930, but he refused to admit a weakness or to "coddle" himself. Despite his efforts he could not continue his practice at his old rate, but he was sure that tomorrow, next week, next year, everything would be all right. I always felt an apprehension in the back of my mind after the day in winter when we had gone out to do some pruning. We were working along a southerly slope where even the low sun was warm, when he suddenly staggered off his ladder and sat down on the frozen ground with his head between his knees. I perched on my ladder, paralyzed with fear at an action so uncharacteristic, so strange. After a while I climbed down and stood beside him where he sat without moving, his face flushed and almost purple, and asked him what was the matter.

"Just dizzy," he said. "I have been having these spells lately. Imagination probably. But I think I won't do any more just now." Finally he got up, and we went slowly back to the house. Several times he stopped and examined the buds on the tips of the branches. "It will be a good crop, the best yet," he said.

It was during this time that he put another mortgage on the farm. He said he had been told it was sound business to have a mortgage, and a good apple year would take care of it easily.

The autumn of 1931 saw the trees loaded. Two days before we were to start picking, a great black cloud rolled up in the north. Home for the harvest, I stood by the barn watching it.

There were dark mountains lanced with lightning and, below them, rolls and whirlpools of what looked like dirty wool: a portentous and angry sky. With the first icy blast came the hail, lashing across the trees that seemed to twist and cower. For ten minutes the hailstones poured down, piling up into shallow drifts and windrows. Then it was gone—and so was the crop. We didn't pick the apples. We brought in a few to look at, the delicate red skins slashed in a dozen places and the white flesh already turning brown. My father, who had come back from work looking pale and drawn, said nothing for a while, and then began speaking of next year's harvest.

After my father's funeral, the family—my mother, my two brothers, and I—sat down to decide what to do. Even though I was grown and had been away working on my own for ten years, I felt as though a cornerstone of my life had let go and that the whole structure was tottering. The Depression was not yet real to me; my job seemed secure enough, and I lived as always from payday to payday, with nothing saved to lose. It was not until I saw the mess that things were in at home, where I had thought everything so secure and so unchanged, that I began to realize.

I was like my father. He, too, could not realize, apparently. Even when people did not pay their bills and his practice fell off, he could deny his family nothing, nor change his way of living. When college bills came due, he simply put more mortgage on the farm. When his health began to fail, he ignored it, and life went gaily on. Tomorrow, next week, next year . . . and in the last analysis, he assured us, the farm would take care of everything. Meanwhile, there was no money to pay the bills.

In the family discussion I stood alone for keeping the farm. No one shared my optimism that it would "take care of everything." I could not imagine life without it: no center for the existence of the family, no link with the past. It was in the feeling, I think, that somehow I could keep the past alive and save something of the old happy days that I urged and argued until the family agreed to let me try to keep the farm from foreclosure.

And so all of us went our separate ways, each bearing his burden of the bills to be paid off, and I was left alone. I had never been alone in the house before, but for a while after they had gone I felt relieved, glad that there was an end of argument. "Let the bank take it," they had said. "Let's get rid of it—with its unpaid bills, its hailstorms, its insect pests (each year something new!), its leaky roof, and salty well." I myself had little knowledge of farming—basically what I had absorbed through my pores ever since I was a child and what I had learned during vacations working in the orchard. Yet not for a moment did I agree with the rest of the family that the most hopeless thing in all our hopeless muddle was the farm.

Right then, there was nothing much to do. I had burned my last bridge by sending a telegram to my employer at the Hartford Museum saying I would not be back. I went up to the room that had been mine since my grandmother died. Three decades earlier I was born in that room, which still had the wallpaper with the yellow roses. It had always been a place of refuge; no matter what happened, I always felt better if I knelt down on the cricket by the southwest window and, with my chin on the sill, looked out across the wide expanse of marshes. I did this again as the numbness began to wear off and I felt the ache returning. Once again, it worked.

The window at which I knelt looked into the trees and over the top of the old purple lilac, out to the southeast toward the hills of Essex and West Gloucester. The marsh was like a bay of emerald grass, washing against the upland with its gently sloping hayfields, patches of oak, and old stone walls half-hidden by hedgerows of chokecherry and shadbush. Everywhere the marsh was veined with saltwater creeks, and at the foot of our hayfield a wider creek, an arm of the sea really, rolled deep and sometimes rough at high tide. At low water it was an expanse of mud and sand flats. Countless times my eyes had followed the clammers' dories rowing down the narrow channel or watched the men at work, looking like bent hairpins in the distance.

Feeling the smooth paint of the sill under my chin, I remembered how amazed I was as a little girl, when suddenly I realized that I could call up the exact tones of a person's voice, could entertain myself when I was alone by picturing and examining a past scene in minutest detail: the expressions on people's faces, cranberry vines on the damp sand of the beach, the pepper-and-salt coat of Nixie, the family dog who died when I was five.

I had learned the art of seeing from my father. Faced all his life with the threat of blindness, he began in middle age to cultivate what he called his "inner eye," and in order to keep it fed with impressions, he studied with intense concentration the world around him. When we worked with pruning saw and shears in the orchard on winter afternoons, he studied the apple buds—how they lay close to the twig, folded tight, protecting the green heart of the spring leaf against the cold of winter. Or the triple bud of the peaches, in which were hidden the deep pink flowers that would precede the leaves when the warm winds blew and the snows melted. The tiny things he observed with his nearsighted eyes from inches away, staring and staring, impressed their every detail on his inner eye. The vast sweeps of distance, of sky and marsh and sea, to him were blurred and seen through a perpetual mist, but to my sharp, young eyes, they were clear in detail. I, too, practiced looking, and for my reward I could at any time recall faces and even whole scenes from years ago.

Now I cautiously tried to see my father's face and hear his voice, but the effort brought a pain breathtaking as a stitch in the side. Instead I recalled my grandmother, his mother, gone now so many years that the ache of her passing had vanished. Feeling her there beside me, in her rocking chair by the window, imagining that she was embroidering as she did every afternoon following a morning of work on the farm, made me feel better. I dwelled on details of a morning we might have spent, letting the cows out to pasture after they had been milked, leading old Billy and Sugar, the horses, to the watering trough. I could see the bright drops on the hairs of their chins as they raised their heads. We gathered the eggs and mashed hard-boiled ones for the baby chicks in the brooder; we undertook a bout of weeding and hoeing in the black earth of the vegetable garden, and picked some strawberries for lunch.

I wanted to preserve what we'd had, even though the animals were no longer there, and it was apples now. Later, lying in my bed in the quiet house, I thought about the next harvest, the one my father had staked his hopes on. I went over the afternoon's argument and I still felt differently from the others in my family. I pictured the trees loaded with fruit, the familiar fields well tended, and most of all, the house a gathering place for family and something left of the old days. I was sure it could be done, and I turned over and went to sleep.

In the morning I walked out with Freya into the orchard under the warm spring sun. I still could not bear to think of my father. I did not want to look at his pruning saw and hat where he had left them. The buds were swelling on the trees, and it was close to time for the first insecticide spray, before the outside leaves separated and grew "big as a squirrel's ear."

In the barn the tractor crouched rusty and crusted with mud, just where last summer's hired man had left it. Behind it was the sprayer, a two-hundred-gallon barrel-shaped tank on two heavy wheels. On top was a single-cylinder motor that pumped the pressure for the spray and also mixed the poisons. It had to run all the time or the mixture would settle and begin to solidify; then the granules would plug the fine nozzle of the hose.

Now it looked as though it would never run again. A long stain of ominous green ran from the brass-lined pump down the side of the barrel; the motor was red with greasy rust. I climbed up, lifted the small square hatch, and peered into the tank. There were six inches of murky liquid in the bottom, last summer's spray, never washed out. It had not split the tank when it froze in the cold barn, but what it must have done to the expensive lining of the pump! The green stain showed that. If the tractor engine was as bad . . .

In the stack of unpaid bills, I came upon one from last year: the charge to get the tractor running then had been two hundred dollars. What would it cost now? I engaged the crank and heaved. It wouldn't budge. A little rusty, maybe. I braced myself and with all my strength yanked and jerked and cursed. I couldn't turn it over. In a sweating fury I hauled out the oil stick and looked at it. Dry. The tractor must have crawled into the barn overheated and frozen when it cooled. Lucky that hired man didn't poke his stupid face in at that moment.

Perhaps it was a good thing to start off in a rage. There was no time for mooning and grieving for what was gone. The frenzy of determination of that awful moment was strong enough to last for many months, although toward the end it deteriorated into a bulldog's hanging on. While my anger was red-hot it was fine, a sweeping, fiery current that bore me rushing along and burned away every obstacle.

In the savings bank I had a little secret stake, about fifteen hundred dollars, all that was left of the proceeds of the sale of a yawl I had once owned. I had never saved anything from any of my jobs. When the stock market crashed in 1929 and all my fellow workers were cursing and crying over the loss of their savings and the disappearance of fortunes that they had made on paper, I was very smug. I had nothing to lose.

The yawl had been my most tremendous extravagance. She had cost five thousand dollars, trickled out from my weekly pay over a long period of time. Still, I felt I had got my money's worth in one wonderful cruise down the Maine coast, where I could hardly bear to let anyone else take the wheel, even for a moment, and sat hour after hour grasping the smooth mahogany spokes, feeling my little vessel respond to the least variation in the wind, delighting in the curve of the high Marconi mainsail, like a gull's wing against the sky. After that, my job took me away from the sea, and the *Myth* lay idly at anchor. Even I could see that it was silly and expensive to keep her, and so she was sold. I watched the big triangle and the little triangle of her still-new sails disappear behind the island on their way to the sea before I turned sadly away.

I had almost thrown all that was left of the yawl into the pot several times, but some unusual caution had stayed my hand and now I had the stake. I decided to portion it out bit by bit on some of the more pressing bills so that I could run up bigger ones. I made up my mind that I would tell the creditors how things were and use the payments as evidence of my good will. I didn't know whether they would take a chance on me, but I hoped they would.

I went first to the garage where the tractor and spray engine had been repaired the year before. To the owner, neat and formal in his business suit, I must have come as a shock, covered with grease and gray slime from the sprayer, with a barked knuckle (gained in the angry struggle to open the tank drain plug with a wrench) still oozing through the crust of dried blood. I plunked down one hundred dollars "on account"; I owed him three hundred. He accepted it politely and put it in the drawer.

We sat down. He didn't know me nor I him, but I didn't feel shy or embarrassed. At the time the whole deal seemed quite reasonable. I should succeed, of course; there was just the little matter of getting started.

"This is the way it is," I said, very businesslike. "A city bank that holds the mortgage wants the farm, and so do I. The interest is paid to date, and I shall keep it paid. The rent of the house will take care of that until the crop comes in. If the bank should take the farm, I suppose you would get all your money right away, but we have had the place for a long time, and it is the only thing that can be salvaged from our wreck. It is quite a wreck, as you probably know." He nodded. Everybody knew, apparently. Well, that made it easier; no more explanations were necessary.

"I should think it would cost five hundred dollars to get the machinery running, maybe more. Will you fix it and take a chance? I think I shall be able to pay for it in November, but if you don't want to wait, say so. I shan't blame you a bit, and I shall certainly understand."

He didn't even hesitate. "I'll have a man down there this afternoon. Don't worry, we'll get her running."

The little French mechanic swore under his breath as he looked the tractor over. "Don't look like they put any oil in her all summer," he said. "Oh sure, she'll be okay. Take a week maybe. Cost some dough. You want to be careful when you're pulling stumps with this thing and doing heavy ploughing. You see those front wheels come off the ground, you quit pulling, and quick. They rear right up sometimes and fall over on you. Just watch those front wheels. Lots of work in this baby yet.

"That spray engine," he went on, "she's a mean little bastard even when she's right. Awful hard to start, but once she's running she keeps running. She's not too bad. Won't take long to fix her up. But you better get someone down to look at that pump. Your father used to have fellers from where he bought the thing. Up near Boston someplace. You know where?"

"Yes," I said, "I know." I had a bill from them, too.

The sprayer was fabulously expensive to fix. The whole brass lining of the pump was eaten away by the corrosive chemicals. For a while I thought of throwing my whole bundle into buying a new rig, but the idea of not having a cent of capital was something I couldn't face, so we patched up the old one, and it lasted in the orchard as long as I did.

Once again something was left on the old bill while I was trusted to run up a new one. In those years I found that the proportion of nice people to stinkers was about ten to one. After I had had ten good breaks I began to watch out for the eleventh.

Usually this was the man from the bank that held the mortgage. He always drove his Cadillac into the yard when I was in some sort of a mess with a balky engine or hurrying to get the trees sprayed in the face of a rising wind. He generally began by complaining that I was allowing "the bank's property" to run down, mentioning that if this state of affairs was allowed to continue I should have to begin paying something on the principal to protect the "bank's equity." I used to stand before him, furious—sweating, dirty, and miserable, aware of the fresh tankful of spray settling and congealing down in the orchard.

The discussion always ended on the same note: The property looks run down; you will have to put a new roof on the house. And my saying I plan to spend something on the upkeep in the fall; how much I can do depends on the crop. And his talking about taking steps. What steps? Instituting foreclosure proceedings. He never got out of the car, but he took in everything and viewed it and me with cold disapproval. On my side I detested him and burned to tell him to get the hell out. His visits took more out of me than twelve straight hours of spraying; but he was only the eleventh man, after all.

While the sprayer was being fixed I had the tractor to practice on. It had no self-starter, and in the cold of the early morning it started awfully hard. I had to spin it and spin it until my throat was dry and my mouth bitter with salt. When I was at the end of my rope I gasped out loud, "Just once more," and she would roar into life as nice as you please and chug along the rest of the day.

It was fine to perch up on the hard seat and rattle away over the fields where the hopeful green blades were beginning to poke up through the fog of last year's grass. Song sparrows sang in the hedges along the stone walls, and the red-winged blackbirds cheered in the lowlands. The late April sun was hot; but a breath of east wind drifted an occasional wisp of fog past the budding oaks of the island, and offshore the lavender fog bank lay waiting to move as the sun went down. Freya galloped behind me like a long-legged colt, waving her silly rope tail. Pretending to be a hunter, she thrust her big wrinkled face into woodchuck holes, though she would have backed away in terror if the owners had come out chattering. Sometimes I saw one sit derisively at its back door, squatting like a prairie dog, while Freya snuffled and scratched in its front yard, twenty feet away.

The peach orchard was a mass of fat, deep-pink buds ready to burst, and no sign of a leaf on the slender branches. Below it along the edge of the marsh lay deep drifts of salt grass mulch, sheared by the tidal ice from the thatch banks along the creeks and washed in by the high tides of winter. This I pitched into the rattletrap homemade trailer and piled deep around the delicate trunks of the peach trees to discourage the heavy sod around the feeding roots.

I loved the peach trees, temperamental natives of Persia and China, never really at home in grim New England. Only the presence of the ocean, tempering the air in winter and holding back the rush of spring, enables peaches to grow so far north. The rows of fragile trees, running east and west along the borders of the marsh, even in youth carried the promise of early death. They were so frail, so delicate, that I lavished on them hours of time that I could ill afford, the kind of attention one gives to an invalid child not long for this world. Those five hundred spindly little trees had to have special sprays at odd and inconvenient times. The lime sulphur and arsenate of lead for the apples were too strong for the peaches, burning the leaves and the delicate wood.

They had been my father's pride. Every spring after the fruit had set he went over them individually and picked off two thirds of the fuzzy baby peaches, each only as big as the tip of a little finger, so that the remainder would grow to a handsome size. I continued the practice even though the thinning had to be done at the busiest season, when my working day sometimes stretched to eighteen hours. Later, when I had to prop the branches cracking under their load of oversized fruit, I was glad I had.

At long last the sprayer came back; then my troubles really began. I had missed the first spray altogether, but I hoped it wouldn't matter if I was extra thorough on the others. I had bought the chemicals on credit, basing the amount on last year's order. I had studied the timing and the proportions on the chart sent out by the state extension service. Every morning I had walked down through the orchard to the salty well to turn on the pump and watched nervously while the worn-out little engine fought to drag up the water and, wheezing and gasping, push it up the hill to the wooden tank where we filled the sprayer. The cypress boards had shrunk during the winter, and for days water gushed through the cracks. I was not worried. This happened every year, and eventually the boards swelled and the tank leaked no more. After supper when I went down to turn off the pump and give the motor a night's rest, I noticed how each day the buds were growing larger, the little stems separated, the curled petals showing pink at the tips. It was time to spray, and past time.

The first evening that I walked down through the soft twilight I found myself expecting to meet my father among the trees and could almost hear the tones of his voice. I felt the hair prickle on my neck as I wondered what I would do if we did meet again. I thought I should be frightened. But then, thinking about it, I knew I should not be, for he was bound to be a friendly, laughing ghost, and one I longed to see. After that I looked always hopefully, but I never saw him. I concluded then that there were no ghosts, because surely if there had been I should have seen one there.

Finally, everything was set to go. In other years spraying had required two men, one to drive the tractor and one to haul the hose around the trees. I figured to get the bank their hush money by doing the job alone. I planned to drive down the row, stop, and cover everything I could reach with the hose before I moved on again. I knew it would be slow and heavy work dragging the stiff hose through the grass, but it was possible. It could be done.

That first morning I was all through breakfast at five o'clock. In high spirits I went out to the barn, Freya galloping ahead, the birds singing, the sun warm, everything ready. For once the tractor started almost easily. The spray rig on its two-wheeled trailer with the engine and double-action pump on top squatted malevolently in the corner. You had to engage the forked drawbar to the drawbar of the tractor, hole to hole, and pin the two together with a bolt. I backed the tractor up to it, threw it out of gear, got off, and tried. Too close. In trying to move the tractor six inches, I moved seven or even eight. Too far away. I tried to drag the spray rig to the tractor. Too heavy.

Half a dozen times I maneuvered forward and back, wrestling savagely with the gear shift and getting off to hoist the heavy front end of the sprayer. I could not get into the right position. Never have I felt such an incompetent fool. Here we were with time wasting, and I couldn't even get out of the barn. If my friend with the Cadillac had appeared at that moment he could have had the whole business free, for nothing.

At last I gave up the futile backing and filling and shut off the roaring motor. In the abrupt silence as I sat slumped on the seat, everything suddenly seemed quite simple. All that was needed was a stand to prop up the front end of the sprayer to the height of the tractor hitch. I contrived one from a chestnut-wood apple box, some scrap lumber, and mismatched nails—no thing of beauty, but it worked, and I finally drove out of the barn in triumph.

The spray engine was like an old-time motorboat; you had to spin the flywheel to start it. I remembered fishing trips in the double-ended motorboat and how, after we had lolloped around for hours with more or less success, my father hauled up the anchor and then began the routine with the old Lathrop engine. Spin, gasp, and cuss, over and over, my father's face purple with rage and effort and I, a spindly little kid, keeping my balance in the rocking boat and trying not to giggle. The technique still worked. The engine grunted *huh, huh,* as I jerked the flywheel over, started just when it seemed it was never going to, popped and banged for a while, and then settled down to a steady *kerchug, kerchug.*

When I sprayed, the trees looked as though it had snowed: every leaf and twig was coated with the powdery poison. I guess it paid off, because all through that first summer, the fruit stayed clean and I stayed dirty. The sulphur and the broiling sun among the trees burned my skin raw; engine grease was ground into my hands. At night I was too tired to wash my clothes clean; I just softened them up a little from time to time.

Those were days of triumph, and I sailed along from dawn to dark, borne on the wave of optimism while the fruit grew, clean and sound, on the loaded branches. The farm, the beloved farm . . . the trees, each an individual. I came to know them so well. They would do everything—finish my younger brother's education, which my father's death had interrupted; pay off the mortgage and the other bills that so embarrassingly we could not settle. Best of all, they would justify my father's faith in them and confound the doubters. I felt a wonderful surge of strength and pride. I sang and whistled and rejoiced as I rattled along on the tractor. After the long, hot, hard day I fell happily into my bed and woke refreshed in the beauty of the dawn.

*S*ome fine things happened in that first year. After a nasty fight with the bank man over the state of the roof, an old carpenter turned up and said that if my older brother would help him, he would put on new shingles. "He can do a good job, if he's a mind ter," he said, and my brother did.

The old man was quite insulted when we tried to pay him something. "Your father paid me plenty on jobs around here for years," he said, "and I guess I got enough out of him." We had always felt that my father was getting stuck on every job, but no one could tell him so. Anyway, this timely generosity more than settled all the old scores.

It was a miracle when my younger brother, in that Depression year, found three elderly Boston ladies who wanted to rent a place by the seaside. They were accustomed to fancier settings than the square shabby farmhouse, but they loved sitting there overlooking the wide marshes, shaded by two old elms and the linden, which they were fascinated to hear was brought over from England as a twig in someone's pocket. Their rent money paid last year's taxes and insurance. They never complained when water pipes leaked or the rainwater cistern ran dry and left them with only the well water, brackish with Atlantic salt. We had drunk it for years and all other water tasted flat to us, but it was horrible, I suppose, until you got used to it.

When the kitchen hot-water boiler burst, the youngest lady came out to find me in the orchard and said apologetically, "I am so sorry to bother you, but we don't know how to shut off the water. Isn't that stupid? You must show us."

They took the greatest interest in everything that I was doing and insisted that I knock off every afternoon to have tea with them. When I protested that I would not have time to clean up and could only take a short break from work, they said it didn't matter: Do come, please. So I used to sit with them for a lovely half hour on the cool stone porch and tell them all the doings of the day and drink iced tea and eat little sandwiches and cakes. Often when, at the end of the day, I staggered down to the little house behind the barn where I lived that summer, I'd find that they had been there before me and left some goodies in a napkin for my supper.

One June day I had just finished a tank of spray and was coiling up the hose when I saw Miss Rosamond in her gray print dress hurrying down through the trees.

"Something is happening to your bees!" she called. "I saw what I thought was an old sweater hanging on a bush, and it was a great solid big cluster of bees all hanging together. Could it be a swarm, do you suppose?"

That's just what it was.

There have to be bees to pollinate the blossoms and set the fruit, and in any orchard of any size the bumbles and the little wild black bees that are always around cannot take care of the job. Also, they feel no obligation to work on apples and will take what is nearest. Once they have started on one particular kind of flower, they will stay with it until that nectar resource is exhausted. Never mind if the orchard is in full bloom and the petals beginning to blow down like a drift of pink snow. So there has to be a surplus of bees or the crop comes to nothing.

We had fifteen hives of Italian honeybees with gold-striped bodies: temperamental girls, quick to anger. Every member of the family had been terrified of them since the day when my father decided he would get a comb of honey for lunch. He dressed himself up in his regalia: a wide-brimmed hat with a mosquito-net veil that tied at the bottom with a drawstring, a white suit (because white is less irritating to bees), high boots, and elbow-length canvas gloves. He was a fine figure, and we much admired his courage, but we stayed in the house and watched out the dining-room window while he strode purposefully to the nearest hive. We could hear our cook, Jessie, giggling in the kitchen. There was quite an audience.

Bees always seal up their home with a tough brown glue that they manufacture from the sticky coating of buds and tree sap. The top of the hive was fastened down tight. My father almost capsized the whole thing trying to get the cover off, and finally he had to hammer it with a rock. We could see him frantically working the bellows of the smoker, but the bees were around him like a thick mist. We could not tell whether any smoke was coming out. It did not appear to have the quieting effect it was supposed to have, according to the book. Finally we saw him fling the smoker away, the first uncontrolled gesture.

He had the cover off, and we could see him digging at the open hive with both hands, but the honey box also was glued in. Then he abandoned the whole business and, frantically flailing with both arms, set out for the house at a dead run, followed by an ominous, funnel-shaped cloud of infuriated bees. A rising chorus of giggles and squeals marked his progress past the kitchen window. My mother, like a flash, was at the back door ahead of him and locked it.

"Don't let him in here with all those bees on him," she shouted. "We shall be devoured. Lock the side door quick." Someone did.

As he rounded the house at a gallop, some of the bees gave up the chase, but there were still plenty.

"Goddammit, open that door!" *Bang, bang, bang.*

"Shh," said Mother to us.

"Let me in, I tell you! I've got a bee in my bonnet and I can't get the damned thing off. Open the door, I say! Open it, open it! *Owww,* Goddammit. There, he stung me. *Now* will you open it?"

After a while, when all the bees had left the porch for the sunshine and their hive, we did. My father's face was purple. One eye was swollen shut. No one dared laugh or speak the rest of the day, but toward sundown we heard him laughing and cussing, so we knew it was all right. I tiptoed out after dark and gingerly replaced the cover on the quiet hive. That was the extent of my practical beekeeping experience.

After that an old, old man with a long white beard took over. He was always known in the family as Mr. Beeman. Whenever the bees swarmed he had to be fetched from his farm twelve miles away, and meanwhile someone had to sprinkle the swarm from a watering can until he came. So long as the bees thought it was raining they stayed where they were, quiet. Bees are not really as bright as they have been pictured—and not as energetic, either. No matter how badly the blossoms need their attention, they will not work if it is drizzling or cloudy or chilly. Often a crop is lost for lack of sunshine while the trees are in bloom.

I used to follow Mr. Beeman around at a safe distance and learned quite a lot of theory from him. He could quote pages of Latin and Greek relating to bees. Methods did not seem to have changed much since Horace's time, although it is easier to take the honey out of modern hives than from old-fashioned straw skeps. I was cautiously interested, but Mr. Beeman's approach to the subject was a little too sentimental for me. I have seen him gently pick off a worker whose stinger was sunk vindictively into his forearm with the remark, "Naughty little lady, she just doesn't understand."

He often did not wear a net and went quietly about his work with his whiskers full of bees, roaring and struggling and stinging. It was plain to see that the pictures in the bee books of keepers covered with gently crawling insects, and never a sting, are grossly exaggerated; or else the bees are drugged. I think everyone gets stung. Mr. Beeman said it was good for his rheumatism.

Now, without the benefit of Mr. Beeman, I had to collect the swarm that Miss Rosamond had found. Coming up from the orchard, I half-hoped the bees had flown away; not really, though, because we needed every available pollinator. "A swarm of bees in May is worth a load of hay," Mr. Beeman used to say; and this one, in June, was valuable, too. Later swarms are small and don't have the workers to store enough honey to see the colony through the winter.

From a safe distance, Miss Rosamond pointed out the swarm—a solid cone of insects nearly two feet long. They did look like a sweater, hanging on a lilac branch about five feet off the ground. From a distance they seemed to be motionless, but as I drew nearer I could see that the ones on the outside of the mass were crawling over the inner layers, which were hanging together. Somewhere in the middle of the mass was the queen. From time to time two or three others would take off. These were the scouts, out to locate a new home. Once they came back with a satisfactory report, the whole mass would rise up like a cloud and be gone. There was no time to waste, since there was no one to sprinkle water over them while I got dressed.

In the barn, climbing into the white coverall that was miles too big, my heart beat fast, and I fumbled with the fastenings. I stamped my feet into the rubber boots, untangled the knotted string of the veil that was fastened to a broad-brimmed hat, and pulled the whole contraption on awkwardly, then found both elbow-length canvas gloves and laid them out side by side. After a search I rooted out the rusty smoker and an empty hive complete with eight frames of comb, the hexagonal cells ready for honey and pollen and nursery.

The smoker is a can with breathing holes on the bottom, a bellows on top, and a stubby spout. It is the beekeeper's only weapon against the thousands of infuriated insects whose stings in great quantity can mean death. Mr. Beeman told me of a farmer who kept his bees in a room in the barn—not in hives, but allowing them to build their combs from floor to ceiling as they wished. One day he went into the room, leaving the door open, and set up a stepladder to get something from a shelf. He was found dead. Evidently while trying to catch the door as it blew shut, he had upset the stepladder and, in his fall, knocked down one of the immense combs. The bees stung him to death even before he could rise.

The valiant bees who will lay down their lives for the defense of the community fear only smoke. This ancient inheritance is supposed to stem from forest fires, the one enemy they could not conquer. The pitiful little smoker, stuffed with burlap, leaves, sawdust, anything that will burn with a smudgy fire when fanned into half-life with the bellows, gives a certain measure of control. At the first whiffs bees become terrified and forget to defend themselves; but there are many bees and little smoke.

Working the bellows nervously, I approached the swarm on the lilac branch. A tongue of flame shot out the spout. The nearest bees milled angrily, and their deep-toned buzzing rose to an angry whine. I backed away, pried open the smoker cover, and tried to spit on the flames that my enthusiasm had coaxed from the contents. My mouth was dry and no spit came. With the bees roaring around me and hurling themselves against the screen wire of the veil, I hastily raked up a handful of green grass and pushed it into the can. A choking smoke poured out, and I blew it all around the cluster. There was a frantic scrambling, a terrified buzzing, then quiet, a paralysis of fear.

I dragged the hive under the swarm. The book said, "Dislodge the swarm with a sharp snap, being sure to get as many bees as possible into the hive. Cut off the branch if necessary." I could see myself sawing off the branch with all those bees on it! Better to build the hive up to the branch on a stack of apple boxes until there would be only a three-foot drop and not so many bees would spill.

I ran back to the barn for the boxes, sweating with excitement and too many clothes. When I returned, the whole mass was stirring, the air was filled with bees, and the buzzing was rising in pitch. More smoke, quick; but the smoker had gone out. Gloves off, light a match, light another, work the bellows. There. Gloves on anywhichway and not secure at the wrist.

Finally the hive was not too steadily in place on top of four boxes stacked catercornered. Now for "a sharp snap." A great clot of bees fell on top of the hive and poured like thick molasses down the side and trickled into the grass. Another clot was left frantic on the branch. The grumble of the swarm rose to a whine, then a roar. The air was filled with infuriated bees, stingers out like swords. From the corner of my eye I saw Miss Rosamond take off for the house.

Wildly I blew smoke around me, but I felt something like a hot iron burn my wrist, again and again, where the glove and cuff had parted company. I felt it, that was all. I was in the middle of a whirlpool, a tornado, and all I could do was stand my ground and blow little wisps of smoke for defense. Then the pitch of the whining roar began to decline. Looking down, I saw the bees picking themselves out of the grass and hurrying in the entrance. Somewhere in the hive the queen had lit and made herself at home. I put on the hive cover and went back to the barn. Six stings on a swollen left arm. No rheumatism today.

It was my hard luck that I was highly allergic to bee poison, because otherwise I might have made a go of that sideline. Mr. Beeman had died at the ripe age of ninety, and there were many colonies of bees in the county that had been under his care. I made one attempt, and one only, at being a commercial beekeeper; it involved more than I anticipated. A prosperous neighbor telephoned me and said that bees had "nested" somewhere in the attic of his house. He reported that with the approach of cold weather, stupefied bees were coming into the upstairs bedroom and crawling on the floor. He said that his wife and daughters had been painfully stung on the soles of their feet and that he would do anything to get rid of the bees. I said I would see what I could do.

I went to the house on a warm day of early autumn, and we held a council of war on the lawn after he had pointed out to me the bees coming and going through holes in the shingles high up near the eaves. Never one for high places, I quailed at the thought of tackling a colony of bees sixty feet off the ground. I had suggested working from the attic; but he was not in favor of that, as he said the house would be filled with bees. He had figured out that they were in a triangular space between the attic wall and the projecting eaves and said that he had seen them around for quite a while, although they had become bothersome only recently. I looked unenthusiastically at the extension ladder he had rigged up and tried to think of some excuse to get out of the whole thing, but short of saying the truth—that I was afraid—there seemed to be no good reason. Besides, I thought, obliging my neighbor might be good business.

I put on my beekeeping costume and climbed gingerly up the ladder, remembering to look up, not down, to avoid the horrid queasy feeling in the pit of the stomach. Once past the third-floor windows, I forgot my qualms as I watched the bees going in and out through a number of holes. They were working and paid no attention to me. The holes were too small to see through, but from the contented humming sound I felt I could locate the colony quite accurately. I descended the ladder and gave that meager report.

My neighbor was the head of a large corporation and used to getting things done. When I said I couldn't see how to get at the colony, he had the answer. "Cut a hole in the side of the house. And if there is any honey in there, you might take it out. We could use it on pancakes and give it away for Christmas presents."

I protested that I was no carpenter and that I would make an awful mess. He said not to mind, that when I had taken out the bees and the honey he could get a carpenter to fix the house. He brought me a keyhole saw to start the cut, a ripsaw, a hacksaw to cut off the nails, and a pinch bar. He thought of everything. On my side I asked for a bushel basket and a piece of wire to make an S-hook so that I would be able to hang all this paraphernalia from a rung of the ladder while I worked. This was provided, and I started up the smoker in case the bees got agitated as I sawed my way into their home. Fortunately they did not seem to be bothered as I began ripping off the shingles with the pinch bar.

At first I worked ineffectually with one hand while I clung to the ladder with the other. Then, as I became absorbed, I forgot all caution and the dizzy height above the ground. Leaning out from the ladder, I used both hands, ripping off the shingles and hooking out the nails in fine style. In fact I probably would have ripped off the shingles halfway down the side of the house if I had not been stopped by protesting shouts from below.

I had a large area of siding boards exposed when I began to cut a hole big enough to enter the blind attic behind the wall. First I cut through one board with the keyhole saw, then inserted the ripsaw and carved away, stopping after every few strokes to catch my breath. It was hard work. The bees were still not disturbed, as I was working well to the side of where their combs were located. When bees are busy, as these were, and the honey is plentiful, they are only irritable when interrupted by an interference with their line of flight or direct tampering with their headquarters. While I sawed away, they came and went, laden with goldenrod nectar and pollen. Finally I had sawed out a trap door about four feet square. Warning away interested spectators on the ground, I pried out the whole section and let it fall.

The sunlight poured into the blind attic for the first time since the house was built, revealing a triangular passageway running the whole length of the house and some of the most amazing bee architecture imaginable. For more than ten feet the space was almost filled with monstrous combs, fastened to the ceiling, walls, and floor with struts and flying buttresses of wax. I crawled into the hole I had cut and squatted on the floor marveling at the work of engineers who had built the structure out of tiny flakes of wax secreted from their bodies.

The groins and arches were contrived to carry the weight of the combs when filled with honey, and each weighed seventy pounds at least. There had been considerable new building during the summer, as I could tell from the light golden color of the wax. Other combs were black with age, but every comb that I could see was full of winter stores, each hexagonal cell neatly capped. The hatching season was almost over, but there were still some cells containing baby bees, tiny curled white worms being tended by their nurses. There were a number of colonies living in the attic, each with its queen and armies of workers, hundreds of thousands of insects and millions of bee hours of labor to build the giant combs and fill them with nectar, a drop or two from each flower.

I hated to think that I was descending upon them like a destroying angel, spreading murder and ruin.

I climbed down the ladder and reported to the family on the ground what I had seen.

"They must have been there for years and years," I said. "I hate to kill them."

"Why do that?" my practical neighbor said. "Can't you use them? And perhaps we could have a hive or two if you would take care of them for us."

I explained that in order to prevail upon them to remain in a hive I should have to find their queen, and it would have to be the correct queen for each colony or the workers would kill her. I said I thought it would be impossible to locate the queens among the swarming multitudes. "No," I said. "If you want them out of there I shall have to kill them all."

"Well," he said, "perhaps that would be best, but save the honey."

"I shall have to get it out before I kill them, then," I said. "I am going to use carbon tetrachloride, which is poisonous. Trying to get the honey out, though, will drive the bees wild and will make an awful mess. The minute I break one of those combs the honey will pour out all over everything. Better let me kill the bees first and then I can get the honey out more neatly and you can bury it or something."

"No," he said stubbornly.

So off he went to town to get a whole stack of twelve-quart pails, and I took off my bee hat and hot rubber boots and rested under a tree. I was disgusted with the whole business and wondered if my gallon can of carbon tetrachloride would be enough. I wished I had never started.

When he returned with the pails we rigged a line with a hook so that I could lower them to the ground when they were filled. I made several trips up the ladder with the pails and stacked them in the attic, and at last I took a shovel with a clean blade and the smoker packed with burlap and leaves. When I filled the attic with smoke, the bees for the first time sensed that something was wrong. Numb with terror, they crawled on the combs, still trying to protect their stores.

I drove the shovel blade into the nearest comb. The thick, dark honey poured and puddled on the floor. I scooped up what I could and shoveled comb, honey, bees, and all into a bucket. Smoke or no smoke, this was too much for the bees. They roared around me in a cloud, or struggled drowning in the honey.

"Here she comes," I shouted, as I lowered the pail. The neighbor had rigged himself up in a makeshift costume. He stood his ground bravely as the bees followed the bucket down, screaming with rage. His wife and daughters had sought refuge on the porch, where they were safe behind the screen and could still have a good view of the goings-on.

The pail hit the sill of the window on the second floor, tilted, and the honey and comb poured down the side of the house. Some of the bees paused and tried to salvage something from the wreck. The others, in a cloud, followed the bucket down. Hastily my neighbor released the hook and ran for his life, but the bees paid him little attention: they were only intent on retrieving the honey. They fell into the bucket and tried to swim, or with soaked and draggled wings crawled onto floating islands of comb or onto the sticky lip of the bucket.

As the afternoon progressed everything was covered with honey. The fingers of my gloves stuck together; the rungs of the ladder were smeared with crushed bees; amber rivulets trickled down the sides of the house; and there were pools of honey and struggling bees in the grass.

Twenty buckets, more or less filled with an unappetizing mess and each with its cloud of frantic insects, stood around the lawn, and still there were hundreds of pounds left in the attic. At last my neighbor, beginning to be appalled and nursing several stings, called up to me, "That's enough." I was at the end of my rope, exhausted, and the constant crying of the bees had made my head ache.

When it grew dark and the last pathetic stragglers had crawled back to their ruined dwelling, I made one last trip up the ladder with the tetrachloride. The heavy gas settled into every nook and cranny of the structure. Very soon everyone—queens, ladies-in-waiting, and all the society of workers—was dead.

I heard afterward that it cost a small fortune to restore the house, although robber bees (my own, probably) cleaned the honey off the shingles and added it to their own winter stores. The poisoned honey of the attic they would not touch, and eventually it was all shoveled out and buried. For years the irregular patch of new shingles on that house reminded me of my first and last effort to become a commercial beekeeper.

It was at a fruit growers' meeting that I met George Sledge, and probably it was my appearance that led him to talk to me. He certainly knew bees and the most modern methods, which he willingly shared. Two days before the meeting I had been stung and still looked very peculiar. As I drove the tractor across a line of flight a bee got caught in my hair. Before I could disentangle her she stung me on the top of the head. The pain itself is nothing, like the touch of a hot iron, but within fifteen minutes the glands in my neck had swollen so I couldn't turn my head. Then the glands under my arm swelled, and soon the arm itself was so stiff that I could hardly move it. My left eye was closed and my ear just a blob. Even two days later I still saw people at the meeting glancing at me through their eyelashes and then looking away. Perhaps Sledge knew what was wrong; at any rate he came up and we fell to talking about bees.

He said he produced and sold honey by the carload, and I pictured an open gondola car filled to the brim with thick golden stuff that moved in a sluggish wave as the train stopped and started. Since my bees never produced more than a few poorly filled boxes of comb honey and often nothing beyond the amount needed to see them through a bad winter, I was interested to learn how he did it.

George Sledge was a big man with a flat face and narrow eyes that sparkled like splinters of glass. He was always very nice to me and very helpful, but I felt that there was something sinister about him. I think he would not have hesitated to murder anyone who crossed him up, and I have always wondered whether he had "cut a man"—his phrase—in the southern state he came from. He never said which one it was and looked at me sharply when I said my mother came from Louisiana and that I had spotted his drawl. He lived with an old New England couple on the outskirts of a nearby town, and his relation to them was peculiar, too. He made himself as free in the house as though he were their son. His bee colonies were scattered over their acres, and he had fixed up their barn loft as a workshop with a lot of fine machinery. He did beautiful cabinet work and made "antique" furniture, complete with worm holes.

The couple always referred to him as Mr. Sledge, but he walked in and out of the house and helped himself of the icebox as though he owned the place. Often he presented me with vegetables from the garden or raspberries or grapes from the vines, and I never knew whom to thank for them. He had a whole stable of prejudices, against Negroes, Roman Catholics, Jews, foreigners, and "damnyankees." His sneering and poisonous remarks were made in a voice as soft as the drip of his own honey, remarks that ordinarily would have brought me to my feet fighting. He boasted of his membership in the Ku Klux Klan and bragged of its exploits and of fiery cross burnings on New England hilltops. Faced with his narrowed eyes and curled lip, I kept miserably silent. I was afraid of him, I admit it; and so, I thought, was the old couple with whom he lived.

Sledge was a master hand with bees. His colonies were scattered around the edges of a swamp where clethra grew. From these sweet-smelling small flowers his bees made a honey as good as that from orange blossoms. As we walked around among the hives he told me many practical details from his own experience. He knew everything that was in the books, too, and a lot that wasn't. He had ten-frame hives instead of the eight frames recommended by Mr. Beeman and the old-timers. This allowed room for larger colonies and gave two extra frames for winter honey storage. By using a special method, moreover, he never allowed his bees to swarm, so they were at full working strength all the time.

The swarming fever strikes the colony when the days become warm and the myriad new workers for the season are hatched and fully developed. Only a small group of workers lives through the winter, clustered in a ball about the old queen. They are semidormant, moving only to feed the queen and themselves enough stored honey to maintain heat and life. On warm days these workers come out and fly around to relieve themselves; they will never dirty their own hive. When, during long spells of bitter weather, they cannot make this cleansing flight, they die in the hive, poisoned by their own excrement. Sledge said that in his experience this had never happened in our latitude. Here, bees that fail to winter die of starvation.

After our tours of inspection we sat in the yard under a horse chestnut tree, and Sledge talked on and on in his soft voice. He told how the queen stays in the hive and emerges only twice in her life: at the head of a swarm to found a new colony, or for her nuptial flight. She mates only once in her two years of life and thereafter lays fertile eggs. Their sex is determined by the workers. So far as anyone knows, all the queen's eggs are identical, and whether they will hatch into queens, workers, or drones, is decided by the shape of the cell that the mason workers fashion for them and the food provided by the nurse workers in careful proportions of honey carbohydrates and pollen proteins. Sledge told me that it was like the secret Japanese diet that develops sinewy little boys into court wrestlers, mountains of fat and muscle.

When the old queen enters her dotage, the urge to swarm infects the colony. The workers then prepare, in the dark chamber of the brood nest, special cells, many times larger than the others, and the developing grubs are fed the royal diet. At the proper time these cells are sealed over, and there the change takes place from coiled white worm to fully developed insect. The newly hatched queens will compete to take over the existing hives or to lead a portion of the workers into a new settlement: a swarm.

Sledge's swarm-proofing technique was to kill the overwintered queen and substitute a new young queen in each of his hundred colonies early in each season. These were mail-order brides, shipped already mated. Thereafter for two months he opened every hive once a week and searched through the teeming brood frames for developing queen eggs. These he crushed; it is easy to spot the peanut-shaped cradles that house budding royalty. The workers, undaunted by this calamity, often begin all over again, but toward the season's end, they give up.

Goaded by their instinctive knowledge of approaching winter, which they perceive as early as August, all effort in the hive is bent toward honey storage. The drones, who have been hatched in superabundance by the workers to ensure the queen has a husband, have spent a pleasant summer sitting in the sun on the doorstep, gorging on newly made honey or taking short, bumbling flights around the hive. Of their number only one has found a mate, and he has not lived to return and tell about it. His moment of ecstasy was his last, and he fell dead to earth from the high air where his existence was justified. The rest of the bachelor uncles are excess baggage, stingless fat boys who cannot even feed themselves.

When the frenzy of preparation for winter begins and the honey flow diminishes, there is no more tolerating these idle fellows. Ruthlessly, two little workers grab each one by the wings, bundle him off the doorstep, and sting him to death in the grass beside the hive. Others are hustled away from the dinner table inside, their bodies swept out with the rubbish by the clean-up squad.

All this and much besides I learned from Sledge. Although I had to dip into my capital to do it, I was so impressed by his system that I went home and scrapped my eight-frame hives for ten-framers and ordered fifteen bred Italian queens.

At last, the queens in their little cages arrived by mail from the South. They were the first that had ever come to town, and the post office workers were fascinated by the royal insects, each with her little group of ladies-in-waiting who had taken care of her on the journey. A bee-sized hole at the end of each cage was plugged with sugar fondant; eventually, when workers had nibbled the food away, the holes would allow the queen's release. Undeterred by the interested crowd in the post office, the workers ministered to their lady. Some hurried with morsels from the sugar plug, which they chewed and carefully fed to the queen. Others fanned her with vibrating wings or smoothed her slim body with their respectful feet. Never, even in the crowded cages, did they turn their backs on her but surrounded her in a protective circle, heads toward her, stingers ready for defense.

Sledge kindly came over to show me the trick of introducing the new queens to the colonies. Like everything else to do with bees, it was not simple. The new queen could not be simply inserted into the colony or she would be murdered at once. She had to be introduced gradually, to acquire the smell of the hive. But first the New England queen who ruled the roost had to be found and killed. Talk about the needle in the haystack, that was nothing to finding one bee among the frantic thousands in the hive. Sledge knew where to look, however, and on one of the middle frames he pointed out the star-shaped cluster of worker guards. There in the center was her majesty, unmistakable, her slim body russet brown, without the vulgar stripes worn by her subjects. She was much larger, more graceful, more dignified than her attendants.

"Don't be afraid of her," Sledge said. "She won't sting you. She saves her stinger for another queen and leaves the dirty jobs for the workers."

He picked her up and held her for my inspection. She did not struggle. Ruthlessly, he crushed her between his stubby fingers.

It did not take long for the queenless colony to become demoralized. Groups of idle workers sat on the hive or fluttered aimlessly around it. The whole routine of work had broken down, but Sledge said they were still not ready to accept a new queen from a foreign land. Their need had to become desperate, and even so the newcomer had to acquire the smell of the hive. As I watched, he selected a frame from one hive with infant bees ready to hatch. This he enclosed in a special mosquito-wire cage with a sliding top. Into it he put the little sugar-plugged cage with the new queen, slid the whole contraption back into place, and closed the hive cover. He said the workers could see the new queen, but they were unable to reach her to do her harm. In the meantime, even her presence would be reassuring and everyone would go back to work.

I clumsily did the job on the other fourteen hives, picking up a few stings in the process, and then waited a week as he had directed me. I felt that all was well; bee morale appeared high and there were no idle workers hanging around. Sledge cautioned me that, when I opened the hives to remove the wire cages, I must choose a time when the bees were busy with the honey flow; also, I should create as little disturbance as possible, or the workers might pounce on the new queen and murder her in their excitement.

Finally the day came and I approached the first hive—from the rear, as I had been taught to avoid having my shadow fall on the doorstep and interrupt the line of flight. As I watched, the heavily laden workers soloed to their landings and hurried into the hive. I lifted the cover off and gingerly took out the screened frame. During the week twenty-five or more young workers had hatched and taken up their duties. The queen's traveling cage was empty, the sugar plug quite eaten away. A new group of attendants surrounded her. As I watched, several came hurrying with honey from the cells on the outer edges of the comb. Best of all, there was the quiet hum of a contented colony; the workers continued to bring in the honey and paid no attention to me. I slipped off the protective screen and slid the frame back into place.

When the last of the old queen's children had died of overwork, as bee workers do in mere weeks, the hive would be filled with the vigorous progeny of the young queen. All I had to do was to examine every frame of every hive twice a month for the rest of the summer to be sure that no insurgent group was tending a queen egg and preparing for a swarm. This had to be done at high noon, when the bees were too busy gathering honey to be much bothered by disturbance at home. So I began spraying at daylight, three-thirty or four in the morning, and resumed at four o'clock in the afternoon, working until dark. A long, long day. If only I could hold out, it was all to the good, for the early mornings and late afternoons were apt to be without wind to blow away and waste the spray.

Sledge cautioned me to keep plenty of supers, the boxes in which the bees store their surplus honey, in the hives at all times. On my inspection trips I added new ones beneath the ones that were filling up, taking advantage of the orderly bees' habit of finishing the super they had started before filling another. I gave up on the little boxes for the comb honey that always used to be on our breakfast table, and concentrated on big combs from which the honey could be extracted. The bees did not like to work with the little boxes: too much time was wasted in gluing and fancy combwork in the small squares. When they were dissatisfied they got the swarming fever and began to fashion queen egg cells.

Following Sledge's system, I had no more swarms, and the colonies were strong to survive the New England winter. Eventually, there were plenty of workers when I needed them most, early in the spring, as the trees came into bloom.

When I look back on that first summer, I don't see how I ever did all the things that were necessary, but somehow they did get done. I was riding the wave of enthusiasm and hope, and in spite of the often balky engines, the insect stings, the spray burns, I was happy.

Although I was dog-tired at night, I awoke each morning eager for the day. As I walked down through the orchard to turn on the pump, I cherished the beauty of the dawn, the first arc of light in the east and the misty shadows among the trees; then the spreading, growing brilliance of red and gold, the blazing rim of the sun lifting out of the sea with the voices of the birds raised in a hymn of joy. I added my croaking tones to the chorus, teased and pounced on Freya when she urged me to play, flattening her chest into the dewy grass with hindquarters elevated and foolish tail lashing. Or there were the mornings of soft rain, the days when the wind blew from the east and all the air was filled with the sound of the sea and the crying of gulls. It was all splendid, and I did not miss the company of people at all.

The apple and peach sprays were finished right on time, and in spraying time is of the essence. The new leaves and expanding fruits must be covered with poison, especially the McIntosh apples, whose leaves and fruits are subject to a revolting fungus called scab. The spores are everywhere and only need a spell of humid weather or rain to start developing. Once they start, as a dirty brownish fur on an unprotected leaf, it is almost impossible to keep them from spreading to the immature apples. At picking time a scabby apple has at best one or more scaly spots that spoil its value; at worst, angry black blotches crack the skin and cause the fruit to rot.

The list of enemies was endless, each in its season. Coddling moths, aphids, red mites, curculio (a pretty name for a hideous tiny beetle especially destructive to peaches), cedar rust, Baldwin spot, and worst of all, apple maggot—the worm of a triangular-shaped fly that hatched under the skin and coursed round and round through the pulp until the fruit was a bag of rotten mush. At night I used to dream of my enemies.

As each one challenged, I had to be ready with the proper spray, and to every mixture there had to be added the wicked burning stuff, lime-sulphur powder for scab. It took three days, with luck, to cover the thousand apple trees once.

I put on seven sprays that first year. Allowing for the days I got stuck in the mud in the early spring, the days when the wind rose suddenly to blow the spray away so it had to be done over, and the miserable days when one or the other machine refused to run, I must have spent a solid month on spraying alone. Down among the trees it was roasting hot. Forgetting the beauty of the dawn I struggled, without thinking, without seeing, savagely concentrated. The two-hundred-foot high-pressure hose was heavy and stiff. It seemed filled with a venomous life, coiling around invisible snags in the grass, kinking and swelling with dangerous pressure or picking up minute particles of scale from the tank to clog the nozzle. When this happened, I had to run to release the pressure, unscrew the nozzle cap, and pick the bits from under the diaphragm.

There always seemed to be enough pressure left in the hose to squirt the sulphur and lead arsenate into my face or dribble it over my hands, so fresh burns were added to the old ones. My hands were so tough that only between the fingers were there raw or scaly spots, but my face and neck were blistered all summer. To add to my troubles, midges, mosquitoes, and biting flies feasted at will when my hands were too busy to brush them off. I tried nets and masks and coveralls but sweated myself into worse misery, so finally I just worked in filthy dungarees and shirt, covering my exposed skin with grease, which helped somewhat. Grim as it was, there were compensations in the pride of the fine clean fruit developing. I had always been wiry and tough, and at night I was too tired to worry about the future or brood over the past. I just grabbed something, anything, to eat and flopped into bed.

In addition to care of the bees and spraying, there were plenty of other necessary chores. Every tree had to be fed its quota of nitrate of soda, broadcast from a pail under the branches. The peaches had to be thinned and mulched, and the grass between them mowed with a scythe. I had never swung a scythe before and almost cut my legs off while I was learning. I never was good at it. I couldn't get the blade really sharp, nor could I master the graceful body swing, but with awkward effort of arms and shoulders I hacked the grass down. To my eye it looked fine.

When the orchard grass grew so long that hauling the hose through it became almost impossible, I bought for five dollars a fifth-hand horse-drawn mowing machine. A blacksmith made a hitch that would hook onto the tractor (a tractor mowing bar would have been fine, but I couldn't afford it). This makeshift rig required two people, one to drive the tractor and the other to ride the mowing machine and coax the slicing blade with its triangular knives over the rough ground. Luckily for me, Charlie, who worked on a summer place nearby, agreed to help me out after hours. In three evenings the job was done, and the orchard looked like a park.

It was wonderful working with Charlie, even just those three days. Although I hadn't realized it, I had missed not having anyone to talk to. Actually we couldn't talk much over the roar of the tractor, but it was nice to be able to look around and have Charlie grin at me from his perch on the seat of the mower. While we were getting ready and after we had knocked off, I found that I had been starved to hear how other human beings were getting on. I drank in every detail of his problems, discouragements, and triumphs with the most intense interest. It occurred to me that perhaps after all I was not meant to be a hermit.

Charlie was a slim, quiet Englishman with very clear, honest blue eyes. He talked about his wife and two small children and his dream of owning a farm of his own some day, but at Depression wages this day seemed far off. His great interest was in flowers and vegetables, and I think he could have made things grow on a brick sidewalk.

"I used to do piecework in the mill," he said. "My people were all cotton-mill workers in Lancashire. I made a good week's pay. Was a fast man, if I do say it. Then I got sick, and the doctor told me that I was just burning myself out. Said if I went back there I'd be planted in a couple of years. I always liked making things grow and had a knack for it, I guess. I'll never make the money I used to, and my wife finds it hard to get along. But as I say to her, 'I'm lucky to have a job at all in these times.' The mill has cut back to three days a week. And even if it was running full blast, 'What good is money to a dead man?' I say to her. Still, if it ever does start up again I expect she'll try to get me to go back there. Likes nice things, my wife does. But I'm never going back. Never. And my boy isn't either, when he grows up."

After this speech Charlie was silent for a while. He was sitting on a box in the barn doorway and I was leaning against the wall, smoking a cigarette. He stroked Freya's head for a minute, and then said quietly, "It's none of my business, but I think you'll burn yourself out if you go on this way. It's too much for any person to do, man or woman. I don't see how you've kept it up this long. The place looks good, better than it has for a long while, but I don't think you can stand the pace. You'll have to have help."

I said, "I've been beginning to think that, too, but I just don't see how it can be done. Sometimes I feel this place is just the wrong size, too big for one, and not big enough for two."

"Probably so, the way it is now," he agreed. "But you've got quite a bit of good land not producing anything. Why don't you think about a couple more crops?"

"What, for instance?"

"An acre of asparagus, maybe. That grows fine here. It's a salt marsh plant, you know. It would bring in cash when you need it, in the spring. What about some raspberries? Most of their care would come in your slack season, and they aren't too fussy about where they grow."

"More work? I've got too much now!"

"Yes, but you're going to have help, don't forget."

"If I could have you, it would probably be all right," I said, "but I couldn't ask you to take such a gamble. You are pretty well set where you are."

"That's right, it couldn't be me. If I were single I would take the chance and glad to, but I can't do it now. Still, there must be someone with all the people out of work. I'll keep an eye out. Well," he said, getting up off the box, "I've got to be getting home."

"Thanks an awful lot for the help and the advice," I said.

The breakfast dishes were in the sink when I came into the kitchen: one cup, one plate, one spoon, and a frying pan on the cold stove, filled with congealed grease. There were only a few sticks of wood in the woodbox, and I hadn't had time to clear out the ashes. I took a box of crackers off the shelf. They were soggy but not too bad. I poured myself a glass of milk and took them out to the porch.

The cottage where I stayed in the summer was tumbledown and the porch rickety, but it looked into the big oak tree where we had had a swing and a set of flying rings when we were children. I thought as I ate that I felt as limp as the crackers. For the first time I felt a wave of depression and doubt. What was it all for, and who cared? In tune with my thoughts, a screech owl in the oak gave a quavering wail and was answered by another down in the woods.

"This won't do, Freya, this won't do at all," I said aloud. The big dog heaved herself to her feet and came over to me. She thrust her cool nose into my hand. I felt my eyes begin to prickle and shook my head fiercely. "Sorry for myself, now, a fine thing," I said to the dog, and she flapped her tail.

I went out into the backyard, picked up an old board and the hatchet, and began splitting wood, walloping each stick so hard that the blade sank into the chopping block and I had to wrench it out. Suddenly I felt better.

"Well, if all it takes is work," I said to Freya, "there's certainly plenty of that."

Early in August the first of the peaches ripened. The trees had been planted so that they would ripen in sequence for about six weeks. The peaches were all white-meated, rosy-cheeked, and juicy sweet, allowed to ripen on the tree and picked when they were so delicate that a finger touch would bruise them. In my father's day, they were picked lovingly one by one into baskets lined with shredded purple paper, carried to the barn as if they were crown jewels, and sold to epicures who came from far and near to buy a dozen or so of Crockett peaches.

"You see," my father used to say, triumphantly emptying his pockets of dollar bills and change; and even my mother, always a doubting Thomasina where the farm was concerned, had to admit that the peaches did quite well and certainly they were delicious. We lived high off the windfalls, sliced with cream or churned to an ambrosial ice cream in the old wooden bucket with salt and ice on the back porch.

Apparently our peaches were still famous, because people from a prosperous summer resort nearby had been telephoning and writing for some weeks to know when they would be ready and to place orders. These first contacts with the buying public reminded me that I had always hated selling anything.

The first job I ever had was on a weekly newspaper, and in an effort to keep the paper (and my job) alive, I tried to sell advertising space. Nobody told me where to go or what to do, so I started gaily off with the first port of call a big department store in a nearby city. I figured that our readers probably did their shopping there, and it seemed a logical place to start. I was proud of the paper: after all, I had written much of it myself. The publisher, who was sick and discouraged, about to go out of business, didn't care what I put in.

The advertising manager kept me waiting a long time. I sat picking at my brand-new briefcase, feeling my confidence oozing away. Just when I had convinced myself that the paper itself was no good, he appeared and was all too quick to agree with me. Furthermore, he told me I was wasting his time, which was valuable. Wretchedly I crawled out and tackled the next place and the next with decreasing assurance. Some people were curt and cold, some were embarrassingly warm—but not about the opportunity to buy advertising. I felt my face flaming as I tried to parry their jocular remarks. Worst of all, they laughed and made derogatory comments about the paper, copies of which I always produced feebly from the briefcase. I kept trying for about a week, but the last few days I spent much time sitting at lunch counters with a cup of coffee, trying to screw up my courage.

I had hoped selling my own fruit would be different. I knew that to make anything at all from such a small farm I should have to retail most of it and keep the middleman's and jobber's profit for myself. The fruit on the tree looked magnificent. Packed in bright-colored paper in small baskets, it still looked fine. But by the time I had rattled up the service drives of the rich estates in the battered farm truck, it looked rotten. I quailed before the grandeur of the cooks and squirmed when I heard the maids and chauffeurs giggling among themselves.

In an agony of self-consciousness I toiled up and down the back steps with baskets and boxes of fruit, aware of my worn dungarees, my black and broken fingernails, and my burned and peeling face. But every now and then a kindly cook would give me a cup of tea and a piece of cake, or a shirt-sleeved chauffeur would lend me a hand with a heavy box. So I kept on with it and resisted the temptation to unload the whole crop to the peddlers who came almost daily to the farm.

On weekends I set up what I thought of as a "roadside stand," a plank between two sawhorses with displays of peaches and early apples. I sold a surprising amount, fifteen or twenty dollars' worth on a good day, but I detested it. It was necessary to chatter and argue about the fruit and explain why it was better than the cheap stuff in the market. City people in cars seemed to feel that in the country they should get the fruit for practically nothing, since all I had to do was to step out to the tree and pick it. In fact, some passersby were willing to save me the trouble by climbing over the fence and picking the fruit themselves. From my perch behind the plank I could keep an eye on the peach orchard. I probably salvaged more profit stopping thieves than from sales at the stand.

I couldn't watch all the time, of course. The fruit disappeared at night, or in the daytime when I was working away from the road. The fence was broken down, the wires cut, or the posts ripped out of the ground. I tried tying poor gentle Freya in the orchard one night, but she was so lonely and afraid of the dark that she hollered and cried and kept all the dogs for miles around barking all night. Toward morning, I took pity on her and set her free.

One day I stalked a couple of villains among the peach trees, and when I pounced on them I discovered they were two frightened small boys with shirtfronts full of green peaches. I shook them till the shirttails came out of their pants and the fruit spilled out. When I let them go they set off at a dead run. In the afternoon I came face-to-face with the same pair on the road. As they started to sidle by I said, "Come here." When they looked as though they would make a break for it, I said, "Come on, I won't hurt you." Bewildered, they followed me into the orchard.

"Here," I said, "if you want peaches, you can take these off the ground. They are ripe and ready to eat."

When they still hesitated I picked up some fruit and put it in their hands.

"Now, you can have the peaches from the ground any time, and if you want apples you come to me, and I'll give you some of those, too. And tell your friends. But I am trusting you not to touch the trees. Okay?"

"Okay," they said, and so it was. The same pair of boys came to me breathless one day to say that four men in a car had stopped by the apple orchard fence and gone through carrying burlap bags.

I ran zigzagging down through the orchard to head them off and caught them red-handed, three in a tree shaking the branches and one on the ground picking up the fruit. I was too furious to hesitate.

"Come down out of that, damn your soul," I shouted. And they did. It was surprising to find how a furious farmer on his own land has the psychological advantage of a little dog in his own yard: he can chase away a pack of marauders that outweigh and outnumber him.

"Now you leave those bags of apples right there and get out of here," I ordered. Following them as they slunk out through the broken fence, I deliberately walked around and took the number of their car. They never said a word, just drove off fast.

I gave the number to the chief of police and said I would appear against them in court, but I never heard anything further; probably they had friends somewhere. The police were never much help to me, all alone near the end of the road, four miles from town. By fall, I figured I had lost more than a hundred dollars' worth of fruit and four peach trees, broken to the ground.

Labor Day saw the last of the peaches, and I had five hundred dollars in the bank. This looked fine and I tried not to remember the fifteen hundred dollars owed. None of my creditors had pushed me and surely, surely the heavy crop of apples would take care of everything and leave enough to feed me through the winter and to start out clear in the spring. In the meantime, at least I could afford to hire men to help pick them.

With qualms I saw the tenants go. I was stabbed with lone-liness the first time I passed the stone porch at teatime. No friendly hail, no cup of tea, no interested questioning as to the day's doings. They had been like family, and now they, too, were gone.

The sun was sliding toward the south. The early mornings were dark, and in the afternoon the shadows lay long across the marshes. On the trees the beautiful, highly colored fruit glowed among the already yellowing leaves.

There was about a week between picking the last of the peaches and beginning on the apples, a heavenly time with very little to do. I spent a day or two moving out of the little house behind the barn and setting up winter quarters in the farmhouse. I would not go back to my own room overlooking the marshes, I decided; it would be impossible to keep it warm without running the furnace. There was no money for coal. Regretfully, I abandoned the whole sunny front of the house and set up my headquarters in the kitchen. Just above it, at the top of the back stairs, was a little cell for me to sleep in, and next to that a bathroom where I thought I could keep the pipes from freezing by using a kerosene pillar stove.

The kitchen was a big room with four windows. Two over the sink looked to the east into the hawthorn tree and a tangle of neglected spirea bushes. The west windows faced the flower garden that had once been my mother's pride, neglected now and filled with weeds. Still there were cosmos on feathery foliage and chrysanthemums, coppery red and yellow. I dragged the kitchen table under these windows and placed a chair so I could see the linden tree, the syringa, and the lilac hedges beyond. To the northwest there was a grove of pines and spruce, planted long ago by my father to break the sweep of the winter wind. They and the shoulder of the hill hid the setting sun, but I could see the dawn from my cot upstairs.

I stashed my meager stocks of food in the kitchen closet and put up some hooks to hang my work clothes in what had once been the laundry. There were soapstone tubs and, in a corner, a wheezy electric pump that dragged up rainwater from the cistern. There were six doors in the kitchen—to the closet, the laundry, the outside entry, the pantry and front of the house, the woodshed, and the back stairs—so I could not manage much in the way of interior decoration to hide the cracked and dun-colored plaster walls. I dragged in an old sofa and set it up near the stove, facing the windows and the table. The final touches to my living quarters were a small bookcase, in which I kept my latest "borrowings" from the library in the front part of the house, and my grandmother's rocking chair, brought down from my old room. Freya thought the sofa was fine and immediately appropriated half of it for herself.

I was still so wound up from the summer schedule that I could not, as I had hoped, relax for a few days. Instead of sleeping the clock around I woke up at dawn as usual and, after breakfast, walked restlessly through the orchard, looking over the crop and trying to estimate how many boxes of apples there were on each tree. The sun had already lost its power. Day after day was clear, windless, and bright, with hardly a cloud. At noon I carried a sandwich out under the trees and afterward dozed for a while in a pile of mulch.

Even though it had baked all summer in the sun and been washed by the rain, the mulch still smelled of the salt marsh. As I lay still, looking up at the sky through half-closed eyes, I remembered my sailboats and gliding through the salt creeks. Other children, my companions of those days, now grown-up and gone, had had sailboats, too. We used to sail in the safe, sheltered waters, picnic on the beach and the islands, race before the strong, warm southwesterlies, or when the wind had died, row home groaning and laughing.

One summer we built a city of stone houses, and I was very proud when the older children delegated me to bring flat stones for the roofs from a gravel island in the river. I made countless trips in the boat I had then—my first, a fourteen-foot half dory—racing to the island before the quartering breeze, selecting the stones and tacking painfully back and forth till I reached the landing where the house builders waited.

My father gave me the little yellow dory when I was seven, and that first summer I was not allowed to venture in it outside the cove, a tiny inlet in the marsh where we dug clams. I longed for the day when I could leave the cove and try my wings on the river itself, with its tides and waves and stronger breezes. That was for next year; and after that would be the bay and eventually the sea itself. The entrance to the sea was dangerous, with bars and breakers, and it was not until I was an older child with a bigger boat that I was allowed to sail out between the rocky point on one side and the spur of beach on the other. Most of the children were warned never to sail through that entrance; usually they were envious of me, who could go freely where I wished.

I had learned to sail with my father in the old catboat, a wild, cranky craft with much too big a sail. After certain experiences in it that, my mother said, turned her hair gray, she gave up sailing. My grandmother went sometimes, but she annoyed my father by always clutching the rail so hard that her knuckles were white and giving vent to what he called "squawks" whenever the boat listed sharply in a sudden catspaw.

When finally I outgrew the yellow dory, he gave me a peculiar craft, a sort of homemade punkinseed built by an old carpenter, the same one who later fixed the roof. He assured my father that she was just the type for these waters; he had one himself, he claimed, in which he sailed everywhere. I suspect that my *Merganser,* for that is what I called her, was really the only one he ever built and that after she did not turn out as he expected, he sold her to us. Shaped like a flatiron, she would not capsize; but running off the wind with a following sea she would dive like the ducks that were her namesake and plunge right to the bottom. I learned to avoid these dunkings by zigzagging, and she was fast and fun to sail.

For my fourteenth birthday he gave me a really lovely boat, a Marconi rig fifteen-foot racing sloop with lines something like a Swampscott dory. Her jib and mainsail were on brass tracks, the first I had ever seen, and she handled so beautifully that it was very seldom that I had to row her home. She would move on a whisper of breeze, even against the tide. We had her for almost twenty years until she literally fell to pieces.

Lying in the mulch pile I could visualize the graceful little boat, riding like a swan on the water, and could feel again the thrill of pride as when I saw her first. It was hard not to grieve for all the pleasant things that were gone. While they were there I had accepted them unthinkingly and without thanks.

As I stood up and picked the mulch straws out of my hair, I thought with amusement that it was the things of my childhood that I had hated and resented that had come to my rescue now. My father did not believe in idling away the summer vacation, so I had to put in four hours of hard work six days a week before I could sail or ride my bike. I thought it was a cruel thing, especially as none of the neighboring children had to do so. I saw them riding by on their bicycles or spotted the sails of their boats on the morning tide, while I hoed corn or picked vegetables, searched out the turkeys' hidden nests, and lugged pails of grain to the stupid birds who would sit and starve rather than leave their eggs.

Early in the morning I had to milk the cows and turn them out to pasture. There were always berries to pick: strawberries under their nets of white mosquito mesh, raspberries and dewberries with their nasty thorns, currants with their worms, and gooseberries with their prickers. I even had to learn to shingle, laying the rows straight with a chalkline and making sure that the cracks of one row were overlapped by the shingles of the next.

Worst of all, everything had to be done right or there would be no sailing that afternoon. I grinned to myself, remembering the job on the henhouse roof that I had tried to hurry through.

The splintery boards were hot and the sickening smell of the hens came up through the cracks. I decided to omit the chalk-line, figuring that I could lay the rows straight enough without it, and here and there I was careless about covering the cracks.

My father climbed up to inspect the job while I stood in the shadow of the barn, eager to be off. One look at his face when he came down and I knew better than to argue.

"It won't do," he said. "It's a rotten job. You'll have to take all the shingles off and put fresh ones on properly. And because these shingles will be wasted and they cost money, you will work all day all next week without pay."

I always got paid for my work, even though I had no choice about doing it. My father said that every worker was worthy of his hire. At that moment I hated him and glared and glowered as much as I dared. I was sure I would never live through a whole week of toil. It seemed an endless time. I cursed and muttered as I spaded the shingles off, damned the smelly hens squawking and fluttering as I stomped and banged on the roof, and tried not to look at my boat riding idly at her mooring. I came in to supper hot, sulky, cross, looked sourly at my father, and answered shortly when he spoke to me. If I hadn't, he probably would have relented. He was a tenderhearted man.

When finally the job was done he looked it over and pronounced it perfect.

"I suppose you think I am very harsh with you," he said.

"None of the other kids around here have to work in the summer," I said. "I don't think it's fair. You might think we were poor, or something."

"There are worse things than being poor," he said. "Being idle and useless, for one thing. Everyone who is any good has to learn to work in this world, girls and boys alike. I'm sure a lot of people think I ought to go easy on you because you're a girl, but idle women make even more trouble than idle men. I don't ask you to do anything that is too hard for you, now, do I?"

"I suppose not," I muttered, "but the other kids don't have to do anything at all."

"That's their business," he said. "You needn't think it's easy for me to keep you working, when you and I know perfectly well that as far as money is concerned, it isn't necessary. I could afford to have you idle away your whole summer and hire someone to do the work, probably better than you can do it. But I want you ready for whatever happens. Suppose my eyesight leaves me altogether; it may, you know."

"Oh, no," I cried.

"Yes, it well may. Why do you suppose I don't read in the evenings now? To save what eyesight I have left. You may have to struggle to get your education the way I did, and I want you to be ready, that's all. Now don't go looking like a sick cat. The world isn't coming to an end tomorrow or the next day. Go take your boat out for a spin. There's a nice breeze."

From that day I viewed my work differently—not all the time, but sometimes. There seemed to be some point in it. I could say with pride and without resentment, "I can't, I've got to work."

As I went through the orchard toward the house, I hoped he could see the trees with their load of fruit and know that I was ready.

There was a really big commercial orchard in the town, Goodale Orchard: a gentleman farm with an impressive backing of cash, judging by their machinery—all quite the latest thing, and new. They had acres of McIntosh, and I went over to see when they were going to begin to pick. In about a week, the manager said. He figured on about twenty men to be hired for six weeks or so, day labor.

"What are you going to pay?" I asked.

"Two dollars for nine hours, take it or leave it."

"How can anyone get by on that?"

He shrugged his shoulders.

"Do you think you can get anyone to work for so little?"

"Think?" he said, "I know I can. I've had about fifty guys hit me up for the job already. They've been hanging around here for weeks. If when they start they find they don't want to work, there are always plenty more to take their places. What else is there? The welfare. They'll work all right and like it."

I was revolted, but I kept my mouth shut. I wouldn't have the crust to offer any man two dollars for a nine-hour day of seasonal work. I had come in hopes that we could agree on the prices we would ask peddlers to pay for the small stuff and the drops, but if I wouldn't hold to the manager's price line on wages, I couldn't expect him to consider me when it came to unloading the cull fruit. I should have to take his price and like it.

We walked out into his beautifully kept orchard and looked at the trees. It was gratifying to find that my fruit was better than his—cleaner, brighter-colored, and of comparable size, although his trees were younger and much better pruned. As I noticed the almost geometrical arrangement of the branches I could see my winter's work shaping up.

On my way home I stopped where Charlie was working. He left the straight rows of his lovely vegetable garden and came over to the fence.

"I shall need five guys in a few days to pick apples," I said. "Do you know anyone really good that wants the job?"

"How much are you planning to pay?"

"I thought four dollars."

He hesitated. "They're not paying that anywhere else, you know. It's two dollars up the line and two seventy-five over in the apple country. My brother-in-law gets three up there, but he is experienced and sort of a straw boss."

"I just wouldn't feel right with myself if I took advantage of the Depression to pay a man less than he can live on," I said. "If the orchard can't afford to pay properly, then the devil with it. Anyway, I think that if guys are treated right they will take some responsibility and pride in the job. I am just not made to hound people, and even if I could there are all kinds of ways of loafing. I can't be everywhere to watch every single apple go into the box. I just think it pays off to be decent, don't you, really?"

Charlie grinned at me. "Sure I do. And if you can get one man that you're sure of, you can pick the others. There'll be plenty to see you when the word gets around what you're paying. Matter of fact, one guy has spoken to me already, Joe LaPlante, a Frenchman. He might be the one for all the time if you can see your way to it. Used to work for a contractor for years till the place busted. He doesn't know anything, not even how to drive a car, but he's quick to learn and a hard worker."

Bright and early the next morning, Joe showed up. He had walked the four miles from town, but that did not seem to be enough to account for the beads of sweat on his forehead. He was not an impressive figure as he stood mopping his face with a blue cotton handkerchief, none too clean—a waste of time, for as soon as he put the cloth away he had to get it out again and do the job over. He was very small, not over five feet three or four, but chunky. His skin was sallow and very dark, his hair black and straight. He kept his eyes on the ground and fidgeted with the handkerchief and mopped and mopped. What was the matter with him? He made me feel embarrassed and awkward. I ventured a few remarks about picking apples and he mumbled answers in monosyllables.

Suddenly it occurred to me that he was just desperately shy. I said, "I haven't finished breakfast yet. Come on in and have a cup of coffee." He raised his eyes, a bright hazel that looked queer in his dark face, then lowered them again and mumbled, "You go. I'll wait. Lots of time. Nothing to do."

I don't know why I said, "You had breakfast, by the way?"

Caught off balance, he said, "No . . . that is . . . well, no. The grown-ups don't have breakfast up my house. The kids, you know, well . . . they have to have breakfast."

"Come on," I said. "If we don't get these apples picked there won't be any breakfast here or dinner either, but there is some now, so let's eat it." He followed me into the kitchen.

After we had finished a couple of bowls of oatmeal and cups of coffee, everything was all right. Nothing like oatmeal to break the ice. He told me that there were six children at his house, three of his own family's and three that his mother had taken in when their parents had died of pneumonia the winter before. "Better with us than in a home, my mother thought," Joe said. "With what my older brother Maurice and I can pick up, we get by. This job will help out a whole lot, though. The only thing is, I hope I'll be worth the money. I never did anything like this. Always pick and shovel, or in the woods." As we went out the back door he remarked, "I always thought only millionaires lived out this way," and life with "the millionaires" of Argilla Road was a joke between us ever after.

As Charlie had said, plenty of men showed up. I recognized only one of them, a young fellow named Carl who helped Charlie out for a day now and again. I knew he had a wife and several small children and was having hard going. In my mind I picked him out as one of the five I would need. That left three more. Then a problem arose.

Four nice-looking Polish boys about nineteen or twenty arrived together: two brothers and two cousins, they said. With them was an older man, also Polish. He was wiry and tough, with wise, sad eyes in a deeply lined face. I felt that he was somebody I could trust. I was touched to notice a homemade mending job on one of his shoes and a quantity of neatly stitched patches on his clean overalls.

The spokesman was Kasimir, one of the young fellows. He beckoned me to one side with a jerk of his head and half-closed eyes. When we were out of earshot of Joe and the others, he said, "We want to work together. We all live in one house and turn in everything we earn. If you take us all we'll come for two dollars apiece. That'll save you half on what you meant to pay and you won't need anyone else."

For a moment I was tempted. Over six weeks the saving would be considerable—perhaps even the difference between success and failure. Of course I was committed to Joe, but maybe I could pretend he was a straw boss or something. This was something I hadn't thought of. In a way it seemed reasonable, and yet instinctively I was put off.

Stalling for time, I said, "I don't see how anyone with a family can get by on less than four dollars. That's only twenty-four dollars a week, and for seasonal work. How can you do it?"

"I told you, we pool everything," Kasimir said. "Like this: My sister works for a rich woman who pays her five dollars a week. Of course she gets her food there, so she turns over five dollars, or sometimes she keeps a quarter for herself. The kid brothers get fifty cents cutting grass or a dime taking groceries home from the store sometimes, and like that. They kick it in. We work a day here, a day there, and we turn it in. We get by. This here looks like a steady job for us."

"How many people are getting along that way?" I asked.

"There's fifteen in our house, three families," Kasimir said. "One family had to let their house go for taxes. The other one rented their place to relatives from the city whose mill jobs closed down. Those relatives get by the way we do, with everyone picking up what they can: in the woods, or a day here and there haying, and like that. They just pay the taxes on the house and, of course, the bank, but while they stay there my cousin won't lose his house . . . that is, if they keep up the payments. Now you see how it is, wouldn't you be smart to take us all?"

I was really stymied, and Kasimir kept his small blue eyes fixed on me while I hesitated. During my own months of struggle I had not realized how other people were faring. Still, the thought kept coming back to me about the workman being worthy of his hire. Even though they wanted it a different way now, I felt theirs was the wrong way. Someday they might hate me for it; certainly, if I took advantage of their need, I should hate myself.

Finally I said, "I'm sorry, I just can't do it. It's a matter of principle, don't you see? I will hire three of you for four dollars, the old man and two of you young fellows, you choose which. I won't pay less than that; I couldn't."

"We won't squeal, if that's it."

"That is not it."

He saw I didn't want to argue and that I was beginning to be annoyed, so he said only, "Okay."

He talked it over in Polish with his brother and his cousins, and as they talked they kept glancing at me. I could not tell what they were thinking—probably, that I was crazy. Perhaps I was; I have often wondered. Anyway, that was the way things were in 1932.

They were nice people and good workers. I hired Kasimir and his cousin Stanley. Louis, the old man, turned out to be one of those refugees from the city who had not been in the countryside since he left the farm in Poland years before. He spoke little English and hardly opened his mouth the whole time he was in the orchard, but he worked steadily, laughed often, and appeared to enjoy himself.

Monday early they all scrambled aboard my truck at the town square and we drove down to the farm. Everything was set: the tractor filled with gas and oil and hitched to the trailer, the grading machine uncovered, dusted off, and set up with the bins in place. It was a good day, bright and windless and not too hot. There had been no frost. The marshes were only just touched with gold. Here and there a sumac sported a red leaf. Every blade of grass was brilliant with dew, and the long morning shadows pointed toward the north.

We were awkward with one another that first morning. I, especially, felt embarrassed. I had never hired anyone or bossed anyone before, and I felt unsure of the right approach. To my eye, the three Polish faces looked blank and the Yankee sullen. But when I glanced at Joe he met my eye with a twinkle and a half-grin, and I felt reassured.

"I am going to drive the tractor," I said. "I don't want anyone else to touch it, not even to crank it. Also I shall have to do all the packing, at least at first; I'm the only one who knows how, and it takes time to learn. At first we'll all work in the orchard and pick as many apples as we have room for in the barn. We'll plan to keep the barn full all the time, so that we'll be able to keep working inside if it rains and not lose any time. This crop of apples is sink or swim for me. I need every cent just as much as you do. I'll tell you right now, I shan't be able to watch you every minute. I depend on you to help me and do the best you can. Now let's get a load of boxes on the trailer and we'll get out there."

There are tricks to picking apples. Each stem has to be snapped off, not pulled out, or the fruit will rot where the skin is broken. They have to be handled gently: fingermarks make dark bruises later. They are picked into bags worn around your neck with straps over your shoulders, leaving both hands free, and the bags have to be very gently emptied into the field boxes or the apples will be bruised. Each little cluster of leaves contains the bud for next year's fruit. Rough handling of the ladders or jerking the apples off the twigs breaks too many of these fruit spurs.

All this I explained as we started the first row of trees. Joe had to be shown only once—Charlie was right; the others, two or three times. Old Louis had a hard time using both hands, but he was very careful. We started out two men to a tree with Joe and I each taking a tree alone. Although at first I often had to leave my tree to help the others, I was careful not to pick just the low branches, leaving the hard ladder work at the top for someone else to finish. I saw that this was not lost on Kasimir and Stanley.

Toward the end of the morning, Joe asked, "How many apples should we be picking in a day, a good picker, say?"

"On thick, high trees like these I'd think fifty bushels would be very good, that is, carefully picked, no bruises."

"We'll be doing our fifty by the end of the week."

"Okay if we smoke?" from Carl.

"Sure, only stamp out the butt. The grass is dry."

I felt fine when I rattled up to the barn with the first bright, clean load of McIntosh. It was swell fruit; grading it would be no job. And they were a nice bunch of guys; everything was going to be all right.

Coming in with a load that afternoon, I found a pea-green truck parked in the barnyard. It was piled with flimsy-looking used boxes. A man was asleep on the front seat with his feet sticking out through the open door; a scrawny boy about sixteen was sitting on a box near the grader; and a lean, thin-faced dark man in torn dirty overalls was leaning against the barn door, smoking.

I backed up my load and shut off the motor.

As I climbed down off the seat he took the cigarette out of his mouth and said, "Where's the doctor?"

"He died last spring."

"Yeah? Well, who's in charge here?"

"I am."

"Yeah?"

At this point the sleeper climbed down out of the truck and started unbuttoning his pants. "Gotta have a leak," he said.

"Shut up, you damn fool. Can't you see it's a woman?" the thin-faced man said disgustedly. "So old he don't know nothing."

The kid on the box tittered. The old man muttered, "Excuse me, lady," and retired around the corner of the barn.

"What do you guys want?" I asked. I could feel my face red as a beet under all the sunburn.

"Want to sell your drops? We been here other years. Always bought from the doctor."

"How much will you pay?"

"Dime. Our box."

I had no idea whether a dime was much or little for apples on the ground, but from the look of the crew I figured it was little.

So I said, "Twenty."

Right away the peddler began to whine. "Twenty—I can get all I want up the line for fifteen, and that's too much. You rich people are all the same: do everything to stop a poor man making a dollar."

"No rich people here," I said angrily. "Fifteen is my bottom price. Make up your mind, I've no time to argue."

"I'll take them, then, if I can have them all. It don't hardly pay me to come way down here for the price, but I've been here other years and sorta know my way around."

"I'll bet," I thought. And I said, "There's one other thing. You pick them up only under the trees where we have finished, and take everything, ciders and all. We only started picking this morning, so there won't be anything for you for three days. Come back in three days and you can have them—at fifteen."

"Ain't you got nothing for today? And us way down here and all ready to go?"

"Nothing today, I told you. Go on up the road to Goodale Orchard. You say you can get them there for fifteen. I'm busy, I tell you, and I want you out of here before I get that trailer unloaded. Come back in three days or not; I don't care."

As I started unloading the field boxes and they dawdled around the truck, I heard the thin-faced man say, "Jesus Christ, what a woman. Things is some different around here this year, I guess." I felt very proud.

But after they had gone and I was back in my tree, I had qualms. Maybe I shouldn't have been so independent. Suppose they did not come back. Suppose nobody came to buy the drops. We would never have time to pick them up, and I had no idea where to sell them, anyway. Seventy-five or even a hundred dollars out the window, and, besides, the fruit should not be allowed to lie and rot. I did not want to go running to Goodale's every time anything came up, to bother people with questions like a know-nothing.

In three days they were back, though, everyone pleasant and friendly. It occurred to me that probably my price was too low, but it was too late to do anything about it. I showed them the block of trees that we had finished and left them industriously piling up drops. For a time I heard the thin man yelling at the kid to get the lead out of his pants, and then I forgot them. At midmorning Joe went up to the barn to fill the water jug, and I saw him come galloping back through the trees.

I ran to the top of the hill where, screened by the windbreak of the spruces, I could see down into the small loaded trees of the north orchard. Sure enough, an overalled figure moved among the leaves, appearing and vanishing. Was he shaking the trees? I couldn't be sure. Just then Freya, who had been snuffling around behind me, spied him and rushed down the hill, barking. She was not brave; halfway down she stopped and stood woofing, looking back at me and wagging her tail. The peddler looked up and saw me, but he was too smooth to act guilty. He just went on moving about casually among the trees.

I was furious as I advanced upon him. "What's the matter? Aren't there enough drops for you over there? You got to make some more for yourself over here? I saw you shaking the trees."

"You seen wrong, then," he said smoothly. "Why, I wouldn't do a thing like that, lady. I just took a walk for myself down here to see what there was. Nice fruit, best I've seen any place. Ripe, too, see?" He innocently held up a freshly fallen apple, the stem still green. "You'd better get picking here pretty soon. Comes a wind, you're liable to lose them. Be good for me, that would, not so good for you."

"Thanks for the kind thought," I said. "You just keep out of here and they'll be all right. They haven't dropped any until today." I should have kicked him out right then, but no other peddlers had been around. The mortgage interest was coming due. If I kept an eye on him it would be all right.

At quarter past five we were going to knock off. There should be enough apples to fill one hundred and fifty bushel boxes in the barn by that time; there was room for four hundred before we had to start packing them out. At three-thirty I was good and tired—we all were. The half-bushel bags dragged on our necks and shoulders as if they were full of rocks. Arms and faces were scratched by the thornlike fruit spurs. It became increasingly hard to get the fifteen-foot stepladders and the thirty-foot extensions in the right places. The high branches seemed to become more slippery and the top dozen apples, always the best ones, more elusive.

Suddenly Joe began to whistle, a gay jazzy tune—first the air, then an intricate series of variations, and finally a whole string of rhythmic changes. The trite little melody became really something, and everyone felt better. The silence that had prevailed most of the afternoon was broken, and we coasted through the last hour on a slide of laughter and jokes.

Driving up to the barn with the next-to-last load, I stopped off to see how the windfall boys were doing. All three of them were hard at it and showed no signs of quitting. The apples were sorted into piles under the trees but none were in the boxes.

"What time are you figuring to get through for today?" I asked.

"I dunno. When it gets too dark to see."

This was something I hadn't thought of. There was not enough time for them to get their truck loaded before I should have to drive mine up to town with the men, and I did not trust them in the orchard alone.

"Don't worry, lady," the thin man said. "I'll stop at the house when we get our load and you can count them for yourself. I always pay by the load."

There was nothing I could say. I hadn't thought to tell them that they must be out when we quit, and now it was too late.

Back among the trees I said, "Can any of you boys drive the truck?"

"I can," Carl said.

"Thank heaven for that. You'll have to drive the others to the square, take the truck home, and pick them up in the morning. Those men are planning to stay here until dark, and I don't dare leave them here alone. It's my own fault, so I can't do anything about it."

After the others were aboard the truck, Joe hung back, pretending to look for his lunch bag. "You want me to stay?" he said. "I'd just as soon. They might be up to something."

"No. Thanks just the same. I can handle it all right. What could they do, after all?"

"Skin out without paying for the load, maybe. You'd be here all alone, no truck or nothing."

"I'll be okay. You go along with the others. It's been a long day."

Reluctantly he climbed into the open back of my truck and they drove off.

I went back to the house, made a couple of sandwiches, and swallowed them down. I had intended to go back to the orchard and just sit there watching until the peddlers had loaded their truck. But, I suddenly remembered, they probably thought I had gone to town. If I could catch them shaking the trees I would have a good excuse to kick them out. Ever since morning I had wanted to be rid of them, but they had given me no real reason. I shut Freya in the house and started out to the orchard. Then, on impulse, I turned back and ran up to the attic for an old target pistol that had belonged to my father. It was rusty and without bullets. I felt rather silly and theatrical putting it in my pocket.

I went around behind the barn and ran up the back of the hill into the windbreak of evergreens that ran like a horse's mane along the ridge. Before I saw them I could hear the clatter of boxes and knew that they were loading the truck. I moved down another row of trees to where I could see them plainly. They were moving faster than they had all day. The bottom fell out of a flimsy box the kid was carrying and I heard the thin man curse nervously and say, "Leave 'em there. We ain't got much time."

My heart was beating so fast that I was sure they could hear me breathing. Carefully, without cracking a twig or moving a branch, I slid along the length of the windbreak, raced down the open slope, and screened by a row of willows, worked my way along the bottom of the hill toward the road. There was still plenty of light though the sun had set, and I moved carefully from bush to bush along the orchard fence. A driveway led down through the orchard to a steel-and-wire gate midway along the fence. The padlock was broken and I had not replaced it. A thick honeysuckle bush grew beside the gate, and I slipped behind it and waited—not long.

The man who "knew his way around" came quietly down, opened the gate, and as quietly vanished. I stood without breathing, not five feet away. I heard the motor start up with a cough and the scrape of branches against the high load as the truck crawled down the rutted track. I took the gun out of my pocket and stepped into the gateway. At the same moment there was a rustle in a bush on the other side of the gate and out stepped Joe.

"Give me the gun," he said. "Is it loaded?"

"No," I said, and gave it to him. He looked very fierce: his light eyes narrow in his dark face, his lips compressed to a line.

"You talk," he whispered. "I'll make to shoot if they get wise."

The green truck skidded to a stop in front of us and stalled. No one would run over two people for thirty dollars' worth of apples, and there was the gun steady in Joe's hand.

"All right," I said. "Back it up."

The thin man fumbled with the starter. No one moved; they were all scared to death.

Joe, with the gun, stood on the running board on the driver's side and I on the other.

"Back it right up to where you came from," I said. The driver lurched into gear and we backed haltingly up the hill. "Now," I said, "unload them. Pile them up, and be careful."

The thin man pulled himself together. "I was just going up to the house with the money to find you," he said ingratiatingly.

"I'll bet."

"No, I was, honest. Got it right here, see?" He held out a crumpled wad of bills. I took it and counted it and handed it back. "The price was fifteen cents, you bastard. Anyway, they aren't for sale now. Get them off there and quick."

Sullenly they unloaded the truck. Joe stood menacingly by with the gun. Once he caught my eye and winked. We were enjoying ourselves.

After the truck with its rattling load of empty boxes had jounced around the bend of the road and out of sight, Joe handed me the gun.

"Kind of useful, even with no bullets," he observed.

"Boy," I said, "was I glad to see you!"

We had a cup of coffee and a sandwich, and then he set off on the long walk to town.

The next morning was enlivened by Joe's account of last night's events, which lost nothing in the telling. I hardly recognized myself in the story, while Joe diminished to a sort of shadowy figure who had just happened by at an opportune moment. I couldn't let it go at that, so I said, "If you had not been there they probably would have run over me and made off with the load. No sir, if you hadn't been there I don't know what would have happened."

Joe laughed. "By Gar," he said, "you looked sharp enough to blow their tires out."

We were all together unloading empties from the trailer. Suddenly old Louis chuckled and said something in Polish. Kasimir and Stanley looked at me and smiled. Then he patted me on the back and without another word picked up his boxes, went to his tree, and said nothing the rest of the day.

The work went smoothly and fast, and there were friendly feelings all around. We covered the big pile of dropped apples with the canvas cover of the grader. I hoped some way to dispose of them would turn up. The day was windless and hot. Toward noon a thin haze dimmed the sun, and there was an occasional damp breath of southwest wind.

"Going to rain," Carl remarked.

"Blow too, do you think?" I asked anxiously.

"Don't think so, just rain, I guess."

"Let's get off as many as we can and tomorrow we will have plenty of work inside."

All that afternoon I was kept busy hauling. Almost as fast as I came back with a load of empties, it was time to load up again. By five o'clock there were four hundred full boxes in the barn, and they were cleanly picked, no bruises, no fruit spurs.

"We'll show them up at Goodale's how to pick apples," Joe said, exultant.

"I guess so," I agreed.

In the night I woke to a heavy shower drumming on the shingles. It passed, and I heard the drip of the elm tree and the gurgle of the rain spout. No wind. I went back to sleep.

In the morning it was pouring. Louis, the oldest, sat in the front of the truck with me. The others huddled under a tarpaulin in the back. I could hear them laughing. The Goodale Orchard panel truck passed us, and I could see the men in back sitting on benches, snug and under cover.

"I wish I had a truck like that one," I said when we reached the barn. "You boys must be pretty wet."

"They can have it," Stanley said briefly.

"I saw a feller works up there last night," Joe remarked. "He said they think twenty-five bushels a day is good picking. When I told him what we do, he thought I was lying, or foolish, or both. Boss hollers at them all day, he said. Don't do no good, though. Boss's back turned, they just fool around. Me, I don't like that. The time goes awful slow."

It was pleasant in the barn. The damp air flowed in through the open doors, fresh and cool. Above the rumble and rattle of the grader we could hear the rush of rain on the roof. There was the busy clatter of hammers as Kasimir and Stanley in the loft converted shooks into boxes. Joe fed apples into the grader and stacked the finished boxes by the chute that led to the storage cellar under the barn. Old Louis carefully placed the small apples that were not packed in paper into their boxes. I planned to pack only the 2¾- and 3-inch apples in the so-called western boxes, for which each apple is paper-wrapped. In these boxes, there are so many apples to a layer and so many layers, according to size; the top layer is crowned up in the middle by selecting slightly larger apples for the middle rows. The finished box is slid into a press that holds down the cover slats so that they can be nailed. A properly packed box bulges at top and bottom, so the apples do not move when the box is shaken or thrown around.

As I pressed one to show Carl how it was done, he said, "Jesus, I'd think cider would run right out if you squeeze it like that."

"It just squeezes the paper. Doesn't bruise the fruit at all. Look, I'll show you." I released the press and pried off the slats.

"Quite a system," he said in amazement. "You'd think it would crush hell out of them."

"It only pays to pack really fancy stuff that way. The waxed paper is expensive, and not many people around here know how to do it. The boss at Goodale's knows. He and I learned at the same time at a big orchard in New Hampshire. My father thought it would help out here if I knew how, and it has, I guess."

After we got rolling, the boys came down from the loft. Kasimir took over Joe's job, and I showed Joe and Stanley how to sort. The grader only sizes the fruit. The apples travel into it down inclined rubber-covered rollers that turn them slowly over and over. People standing on either side of the chute must spy and pick out the spotted or off-color fruit and decide whether it is worth packing later as B-grade or is only fit for cider. There are rules to establish all the grades, but it takes a quick eye to pick out the faulty apple as it rolls down the chute and fast, sure judgment to decide where it belongs. Joe and Stanley were very good at it. At first, of course, a few got by, but I spotted them when I was packing. I showed the men what was wrong, and in a surprisingly short time only perfect fruit came into the bins.

Around midmorning I turned off the machine and we relaxed, smoked, talked, and ate apples. Then we started up again, refreshed, and everything went like clockwork. At the end of the day, we had gotten through most of the accumulation. Last of all we slid the boxes down the chute into the damp, echoing emptiness of the cellar and stacked them up by size and grade. On our way back to town the sun came out.

So it went, day after day: two days in the orchard, then a day in the barn. One morning, instead of dew, there was frost crisp on the grass. After this the sumac and blueberry bushes flamed scarlet and crimson, the coarse leaves of the hickories glistened golden in the sun, and the wide, sweeping marshes changed from emerald to russet. The mornings were so dark that we had to begin at seven-thirty, and by quitting time it was dusky in the orchard. There was a chill of winter in the air. I took advantage of this to cool down the cellar by opening the north door and windows at night and shutting them each morning. The late apples, Baldwins and Northern Spies, were blazing with color, and the last of the McIntosh were dead ripe and dropped at a touch. We soon hit our "fifty a day" and celebrated by knocking off a half hour early and eating ice cream and cake under the trees.

Even the windfall situation was well in hand. A few days after the adventure with the green truck, a man came down into the orchard to find me. "Name's Greenberg, Farmer's Fruit and Produce," he said.

At first glance he was little improvement over the others. He was squat, with a shiny nose and one blind, milky eye. But then he said, "I was sorry to hear of the doctor's death. He was a fine man."

"He was."

"I bought what was left of the crop last year after the storm. That was an awful thing. They didn't even get that storm up at Goodale Orchard, just here. Seems hard to understand, a thing like that."

"It sure does," I agreed, warming in spite of myself.

"You're running the place now, I hear. Kind of heavy work for a woman, ain't it?"

"Not too bad," I said shortly.

"Well, let's get down to business," he said pleasantly. "What do you want for your drops?"

"Twenty," I said.

"Ciders too?"

"Yes."

"Too much," he said, "and I'll tell you why. The market is loaded with ciders. A dime a hundred yesterday and no takers. If I was you I wouldn't even try to sell your ciders now. Just leave them under the trees piled up and run them in with your late apples later on. They'll be worth more then, bound to be."

"But suppose no one buys them then? I'll be stuck with them."

"Don't you worry. I'll scare up someone when the time comes. I don't handle them myself, but I know people who do. The price couldn't be worse than it is now, and it could be better. You don't stand to lose anything by waiting."

"What will you give me for the good drops, then?"

"Fifteen is positively the best I can do. To be frank with you, I could get plenty for ten at Goodale's if I wanted to suck around up there. They're asking fifteen, but I know for a fact that a load went out of there yesterday for a dime. They've got different prices for different people, depending on who you are and how the boss is feeling. I don't do business that way myself."

I hesitated. "You don't have to worry about nothing like what happened last week," he said. "A bunch of thieves, those fellers."

"You know everything, don't you." I had to laugh.

"The kid talked, down at the market. They'll never hear the end of it, scared by a woman with a popgun. Would you have shot him, now, tell me?"

"There were no bullets."

"He wouldn't have run you over either, too yellow. But you couldn't know that."

"Joe was there, too, you know."

"It was you scared him. All he could say was, 'Jesus'—excuse me—'what a woman!' "

We both laughed. "All right," I said. "Fifteen."

And there was no trouble.

By mid-October we had finished the McIntosh and were ready to tear into the Greenings, ten big, low-branching trees loaded with fine slick-skinned apples. "Nothing like a Greening for pies," my grandmother had always said, and my father had set these out among the first. These and the Baldwins were the oldest trees. Their heavy yield, twenty-five years before, had encouraged him to plant the others: first the Spies and later the McIntosh, then a new variety.

There were also five big old trees of Russets, planted for purely sentimental reasons, because he remembered going down cellar as a boy, late in March, and picking a fine juicy Russet out of the spicy-smelling barrel in the corner. Most of the people who appreciated Russets had died long since, but an occasional old-timer still dropped by and bought a box or so. We picked them carefully even though most of them later found their way into cider.

It was while we were picking the Spies that a couple who certainly could be classed as old-timers drove into the barnyard. A tall, thin old man and a frail little old lady were in back of the car, and at the wheel was a bored young man—the grandson of a neighbor, pressed into service as a driver. As I turned around with my truckload and shut off the motor, the old gentleman climbed stiffly out of the car and came toward me.

"We come here most every year to get some of your Spies and Russets," he said. "We're old-fashioned folks and like old-fashioned apples. Had a fine Spy tree in our own yard, but it blew down some years ago, and at our age it didn't seem worthwhile to plant another. I was eighty-five last August, and my wife there will be eighty next birthday."

"I shouldn't have guessed it," I said tactfully. If he had said he was a hundred, I wouldn't have been surprised. He was so old as to be without age. He had silky white hair but his blue eyes under wrinkled, lashless lids were clear and sparkled with vitality. He saw me looking at his hands, brown and gnarled as tree roots, with two fingers missing on the left.

"Lost them in the planer years ago," he said. "Been a ship-wright all my life, and they still call on me sometimes when they need some dubbing with the adze."

"You come from Essex, then?"

"Yes."

He admired the Spies on the load, and I sent Joe down cellar for a couple of packed boxes. While we waited he looked around.

"Things are quite different from when I used to play with the Burnham boys in the hayloft or ride piggyback around the sty pretending we were King Arthur and his knights. By the time the little boys began to play at Yankees and Rebs I was too grown-up for such games, and Johnny Burnham had died at Missionary Ridge. He was a couple of years older than his brother Gussie and me. We never did get to see any fighting, though we wore the uniform for a little while. Yes, things are greatly changed."

I felt a stirring at the roots of my hair. The farm, seventy, eighty years ago. Like yesterday.

"I remember Mrs. Burnham's cookie jar," he said, and chuckled.

"Never could keep us boys filled up, seems like. And the games up attic. We used to try to shoot the squirrels with sling-shots. Most times they were too quick for us. Dirtied things in Mrs. Burnham's trunks, something dreadful."

"They're up there still," I said. "They come in from the big linden and eat their way right through the clapboards."

"It was a great big tree even then. It doesn't seem to have grown much, only thicker. But the elm there, that has grown. And the pasture oak. It's been going by ever since it was struck by lightning years ago. Farmer Burnham thought that would be the end of it, but it's still living, I see."

"It's rent, though, and rotten at the heart."

"Lots of strength to an old tree like that. Five hundred years old, it must be. Goes clear back to Indian times."

Joe had put the apples in the car, unloaded the trailer, and gone back to the orchard.

"I'm awfully sorry," I said. "I have to get back to work now. Couldn't you and your wife come back on Sunday if it's a good day? Perhaps you'd like to see the house again inside, and I certainly would like to hear all about it—the old days, and the very old days when it was built."

"Thank you, we'd admire to, if Fred would drive us, would you, Fred?" Fred grunted something.

The old man shook hands with me. "It's a sad story, about the Burnhams. Some dreadful things have happened here. And great grandsire Burnham told us how the house was built. I will try to remember. So long ago. Goodbye." And they drove away.

All afternoon I was preoccupied by what I had heard. How little we knew of this place: the house, the stage on which for so long my family had played their parts; the rich fields of loam and glacial gravel and clay in which our roots went down so deep. We had been here only forty years, and yet my great-grandmother, my grandmother, and my father had all died here. We three children had all been born in the square southwest bedroom above the lilac tree, had played under the linden, had grown up, and had gone away. So far only I had come back, but the others carried something of it in them. How many family events had taken place here for the Burnhams, way back to 1760 when the house was built? I had been shown a longed-for book, a page had been turned, the frontispiece and a few tantalizing pictures had been glimpsed. Then the book had been closed and taken away. I hoped to have it in my hands again to read. But Sunday it rained, and the weeks went by and no one came.

"When I am through with the crop, I'll hunt him up," I thought. Even though I did not know his name, I could find him; I was sure I could. Essex was a small place.

Meanwhile, on with the job.

By the first of November, we were all done. There were thirty-five hundred boxes of McIntosh in the cellar, of which fifteen hundred were extra fancy, packed in western boxes; the others were ordinary, but all good. There were one thousand boxes of winter apples, a few Greenings, and the rest Baldwins and Spies. Forty-five hundred boxes in all, not bad. If only prices were right. But they were low. It was still black Depression and everyone had apples, especially Baldwins. The market was glutted with fruit from every backyard tree.

"Do you think it will be better later on?" I anxiously asked Mr. Greenberg.

"Couldn't be worse," he replied gloomily. "The very best I could give you would be fifty cents a box for 2 ¼-inch fancy-grade McIntosh. Wouldn't even quote a price on Baldwins. Don't want them. Not now."

"Fifty cents!" I repeated, horrified.

"That's as of now. Best hold them if you can."

I felt sick. At that rate the bank would have me by spring.

I felt too low-spirited really to enjoy our final celebration— home-brewed beer made by Joe's mother from malt and yeast supplied by me. It was good, heady and clear and powerful. Old Louis made a long speech in Polish, very funny apparently. Kassie and Stanley laughed a lot. Joe imitated a jazz band, drumming with marvelous rhythm on an empty box with a couple of sticks. We laughed together over things that had happened and kidded each other until, the last bottle empty and everyone still friends, I took them on the final drive to town.

There, facing for the first time the lonely months till spring, I asked Joe, "What now?"

He shrugged his shoulders.

"I could teach you to drive the tractor and the truck, if you like. It might help you getting a job and certainly would help next spring should you come back—if I am still here."

"Don't worry," he said. "You will be. And me, too, I hope. I never liked a job so well as this one. And thanks, yes. I've always wanted to learn to drive."

And so I taught him, a day here and there, between the odd jobs that he picked up cutting brush or shoveling in a gravel pit or loading furniture for a trucker who had a few hauling contracts. There was an ominous period when he turned up almost every day, always whistling and cheerful, but noncommittal about what he was doing. He learned fast to drive the truck and memorized the rules-of-the-road booklet until he was letter-perfect, but he was nervous with the tractor, afraid of the balky thing. A misadventure on one of his first outings driving it alone almost scared him to death, and I thought for a while that he would never touch it again.

He was very insistent that he should do real work with the tractor instead of just driving it around the fields. We had quite an argument over this, my point being that he shouldn't work for me when I had no money to pay him, and his that any help he might give me would be small return for my time teaching him and the gas consumed. The mishap resulted when I finally agreed and we set about hauling mulch from the north marshes to pile around the peach trees. Going downhill I stood behind him on the axle housing, mostly to give him courage, for I could not reach the gearshift and there was no brake. The trailer with our pitchforks rattled along behind. We piled on a high load, and I planned to ride on top to steady it.

"Take it very easy now," I cautioned. He watched nervously as I climbed up and drove in the pitchforks to anchor the mulch.

"Okay, let's go."

He scraped into low, then into second. The ground was rough and I bounced around like corn in a popper. The engine roared so that I couldn't make him hear, but he discovered for himself in the steepest part of the hill that he needed low speed to keep the cleated wheels from spinning in the loose gravel. He tried to shift and succeeded in getting into neutral. Then the engine stalled, and without a self-starter or brake he was helpless. The tractor started to roll backward, and fast.

"Jump, jump!" he shouted. But I didn't dare for fear the careening tractor would run over me.

He sawed at the steering wheel, trying to keep straight between the rows of trees, and for a moment it looked as though we might arrive safe on the flat ground. But suddenly the trailer jackknifed. There was a crack as the hitch tore out of the wood, and over she went. I slid down, luckily avoiding the polished tines of the pitchforks. But most of the load slid down on top of me. The mulch was dry and not heavy, but there were long, horrid moments while I was buried in the smothering darkness. Then I began a panicky scrabble, and Joe dug like a frantic dog and quickly had me out and on my feet. Awkwardly he tried to brush me off. I was covered with straw like a porcupine.

"My God," he kept saying, "are you hurt? Are you all right?"

"Sure, sure, I'm okay," I gasped out, and burst into a fit of sneezing. Then—at the sight of Joe's small, disconsolate figure, almost lost in the untidy pile; the overturned trailer; and the tractor, crouching innocent and smug—I began to laugh. Whooping and sneezing by turns, I reassured him at last.

He himself had to laugh. "Some driver, me, by Gar. Some driver," he kept repeating. "I thought for sure I had killed you this time."

No harm was done. We replaced the bolts in new holes on the trailer hitch and reloaded, but I could not persuade him to drive the tractor that day. It was almost a week, and then only after a pep talk—part friendly, part scolding—before he would try again on the hill. He never became a real expert with it and was always skittish and inclined to go to pieces, but with the truck he was very good and got his license easily.

Meanwhile, my own situation was desperate. True enough, I had the apples—but you could not pay the bank with them, or the bills either. From the sale of the windfalls to Mr. Greenberg and the ciders at five cents a hundred, I had taken in a little over three hundred dollars. It had cost close to six hundred dollars to pick the apples: five men at twenty dollars for nearly six weeks. This had taken all the peach money and most of the windfall money.

On the first of November, there was eighty dollars in the bank. It was necessary to pay the telephone bill every month; I had to have it, or thought I did. The electric bill was three months overdue, and there had been a note from the town about that. Two hundred dollars in mortgage interest was due the middle of December; the last payment had been made from my hoarded stake, bringing it down to less than a thousand dollars. Not a cent had been paid on the fifteen hundred dollars' worth of outstanding bills. Besides, I had to eat, though not much. Oatmeal, apples, prunes, fish, eels, clams, and potatoes. I swapped windfall apples with a poultry farmer for cracked or dirty eggs. I did have to buy the oatmeal and prunes, canned milk, salt, margarine, soap, and odds and ends, but five dollars a week more than took care of my expenses. The diet was adequate, and I was always so hungry that I did not find it monotonous.

When I pressed Joe as to how he managed, he averted his eyes and said that for the first time his mother had had to go to the town welfare for a food donation.

"The woman there wanted to know what I was doing and how come my brother and I couldn't keep the family from asking charity," he said. He blushed darkly and his eyes filled with tears.

"My mother said, 'Find the boys a job. They want to work.' But she couldn't do that. There isn't any work, not anywhere. Hardly any clams to dig. Nothing."

I could not speak.

At about this time I had a visit from my brothers. They came by train one Saturday. Both had jobs of sorts: one earned twenty-five dollars a week and the other twenty; by living together in the city they got by. We were proud of Mother, who had the best job of any of us—as housemother in a boarding school where she got a small salary, a comfortable room, and good food. But she was far away and confined to the place, and except for her cheerful letters, we did not know really how she was.

I had looked forward to having some family home again. It was the first time we had been together since the day of my father's funeral. I had bought a roast of pork, and we would have the last of the carrots from the weedy little vegetable garden, and, for dessert, a pudding—apple, of course. And coffee. A feast. I had scavenged some wood for the dining room fireplace, had polished the dark mahogany table that my father had brought from Antigua, had got out the unused silver and polished it. We all tried terribly, terribly hard to be merry.

When they questioned me on finances and prospects, I gave evasive answers. I knew that if they understood the perilous situation they would say what they had before, "Give up. It's hopeless. Let the bank have it." So I took them out to the apple cellar after dinner to let them see for themselves what was there. They were much impressed by the number and quality of the apples. We had never had anything like this harvest before, and it sickened me to think that with decent prices we would have been completely in the clear.

"I want to retail all the good stuff," I said. "Jobbers' prices are awful, and if I could sell the fifteen hundred boxes of fancy Macs and the best of the Baldwins and Spies to schools, colleges, and private customers in the city, I should be all set. I can ship them for a dime a box."

Immediately they were full of ideas, so we went back to the house, composed a selling letter, and drew up a list of prospects.

"You will have to sell upward of two hundred boxes a week to get rid of the Macs before they begin to soften," my older brother warned. "And that will take some doing. You'll have to see the college purchasing agents and dietitians yourself. A letter won't be enough for them. Fifty boxes a week is the most you could expect to move through a letter—and that would be a miracle."

"You'll have to call on them," my younger brother agreed. "At least the hospitals, hotels, and colleges." I shuddered at the thought.

Waiting for the train, we skated close to the subject that had been avoided all day.

"We cannot let this thing run down to the point where there will be a bankruptcy and a new load of debt on all of us," my older brother said. "We appreciate what you are doing, but you know it has never looked good to us from the beginning. You are very hopeful and all that, but we think it would be much better to let the bank have it than risk a crash that would involve us all before we've even crawled out from under the first one."

"Some day you will be glad that we still have the farm," I insisted. "Everything will be all right."

"I hope so," my younger brother observed. "But it does not look as if, even with your best efforts, it will be anything we can enjoy for a long, long time—if ever."

The train took them away then, but I felt a crack in my armor and the sharp point of a knife grazing my skin.

Discouraged and heavy-hearted, I walked down the windy, cold platform. I heard steps behind me, felt a light touch on my shoulder. Turning, I faced Joe, dressed in his very best and smiling. Under the brim of his gray felt hat, his hazel eyes caught the light.

"We have a job for tonight, what do you know?" he said. "At the Tiger Club. Playing."

"Playing." I repeated, "Playing what?"

"Playing music. The band. Oh, you didn't know about the band. Five pieces. 'Joe LaPlante and his Wildcats.' " He looked up self-consciously to see if I would laugh, and when I didn't he continued, "We have been practicing all summer. This is the first break. You're just in time to bring us luck. Come listen, will you? It's just a beer joint—no millionaires there. I wish you would. Will you please?"

"Sure." I said, "Why not?"

The Tiger Club was a frame building, built at the edge of a gravel pit, very much on the wrong side of the tracks. A long flight of rickety steps led up to the dance floor. There were several couples on the stairs, and as we reached the top, I could see people in the booths.

"Pray they have a good crowd," Joe said nervously. "They never had a band before, only records. They're paying us ten bucks, more later if we go over well. There are lots of hot spots around, and the cities. . . . this might just be a starter for us. I almost sold my drums and traps a lot of times. By Gar, I'm glad I didn't."

He ushered me in grandly and showed me to a ringside table near the platform where two musicians were already running through a sotto voce duet, trombone and tenor sax. Two other chairs held another trombone and a sax, and beside the fifth one was Joe's gear, the big drum decorated with the snarling face of a wildcat. The place was no El Morocco. The walls were matchboard painted brown. The booths were brown and cream; several of them were cracked. The only light was from the shaded lamps on the booth tables. Above the scuffed dance floor the flyspecked ceiling was decorated with a crisscross of faded paper ribbons.

With a flourish, Joe signaled a seedy waiter and ordered a pitcher of beer—and it came that way, in a glass pitcher with two cloudy glasses. It was good beer, though, homemade, Joe said, tasting only slightly of yeast.

"Let me buy one for the band before you start," I suggested.

"I didn't get you in here to spend your money," Joe said severely. "You're buying nothing. My guest."

He called the waiter over and plunked down a quarter for another pitcher; with a jerk of his head, he invited the members of the band to join us. The two trombones were Frenchmen, Fortier and Bernard, quite jolly and already smelling of beer. The second sax, Williams, looked sick enough to die: cadaverous, yellow-skinned and sunken-eyed. He had hardly enough life to acknowledge our introduction and applied himself to his beer in silence, twisting his mouth as if it were medicine. The first sax, introduced only as Kip, was a real sharpie, a snappy if somewhat shabby dresser. His checked suit, not quite loud enough to be theatrical, betrayed wear at the cuffs and lapels, and his shirt was green with a detachable collar. His blond hair looked marcelled and still showed the comb marks. The whites of his eyes were netted with little red veins, and the beginnings of deep lines showed on his flabby face from nose to mouth and on the forehead. His manner with me was easy and assured; with Joe, kidding. He ignored the others.

"Kip has played with name bands," Joe said proudly. "In New York and everywhere. We're lucky to have him with us. Wrote lots of our arrangements. 'Tiger Rag' . . . wait till you hear that!"

"Your 'Sweet Sue' isn't too bad," Kip remarked.

"Well, what do you say?" Joe asked, getting up. "You'll be all right here, will you? Enough beer? Enough smokes? We'll join you at the break. Wish us luck." And they took their positions on the platform.

The place had been filling up. There must have been fifty people anyway, with more coming in all the time. The waiters were flying around with pitchers of beer, and the proprietor kept popping his head out of a little door behind the bandstand to count the house. Each time the smile on his dark face grew a little wider. The Wildcats tore into their opening number.

The first impression was a really prodigious amount of noise from so few instruments. Everyone was blowing as loud as he could. Even the pallid Williams was flushed, and Kip's face was purple. The blast blew the customers out of the booths and onto the dance floor. After a few minutes the Wildcats quieted down a little and branched into tricky rhythms and complicated harmonies that seemed unique to me.

The band was really good, sparked by Joe and Kip. They galvanized the forlorn Tiger Club into life and gaiety. At the end of the first number there was a burst of applause, and Joe looked over at me, beaming, and raised an imaginary glass in a toast. We had a fine time at the break. I felt like a celebrity at the musicians' table. The proprietor shouted us to a couple of pitchers and patted Joe on the back. Everyone talked at once and laughed. Kip, who turned out to be, as Williams said, "Quite a racontoor," told several funny stories. I left my troubles under the table somewhere and came out into the cold, clear night feeling gay and hopeful again.

*A*dele "Kitty" Crockett
*Robertson at age sixteen,
1917.*

*K*itty at age eighteen.

Dr. Eugene Crockett, Kitty's father.

Crockett House. "I determined that these fields and this old house in which we had all been born would never be lost."

*K*itty at Crane Beach...

and with Freya, the Great Dane.

*A*dele Crockett Robertson, 1935.

The very next day, before the feeling wore off, I went by train to the city to see the purchasing agent of the college. I did not have long to wait for him, which was lucky, because as I sat on the bench outside his office, I felt the well-remembered sensation of courage ebbing away. I still had a little left when he opened the door and asked me to come in.

"I have an apple orchard," I said haltingly, "and this year's crop of McIntosh is the best we have ever produced. Our 2 ¾- and 3-inch apples are packed in western boxes, individually wrapped and delivered to your door on any day you say." I went on until I had got it all out, and then I stopped.

There was a silence in which the tapping of the typewriters down the hall sounded very loud. I faced Mr. Moss across his shining desk. His back was to the light. I could see only the outline of his head, his gray hair, and behind him bare elm branches tossing and a flight of pigeons blown by the north wind.

Suddenly he said, unexpectedly, "Haven't I seen you before? Around the college here?"

"Perhaps," I said. "I worked for the college for five years. In the library. Across the river at the business school. And in the museum. Never in this department, though."

"And now you're selling apples. Well, lots of people are selling apples these days—on every streetcorner."

"But I'm growing them. That's the difference. I like to grow them, and I can do it, as you will see if you try them. But I don't like to sell them. I only wish that someone would drive up to my cellar and pay for them and give me a bonus for their being extra good and go away and leave me to get ready for next year. I hate sitting here. It scares me to death."

He laughed. "I must say you have an odd sales approach," he said. "In the first place you haven't even mentioned price, and that's quite an important item. And before you do, let me say I never haggle. Don't believe in it. You know what your fruit is worth to you, I know what it's worth to me. Now, what's your price in lots of fifty boxes, delivered?"

"Two and a quarter," I said flatly.

"All right," he said without hesitation, and the thought flashed through my mind, "Should I have said two and a half?" No, because he went on, "That's top price and I expect top quality. This first order is a trial. If the quality is not up to scratch, it will be the last. If they are right you can have the rest of the business. We use one hundred boxes a week in all our dining rooms. We pay monthly. Ship me fifty tomorrow."

I made no more calls that day but rushed home by the first train, called up the expressman, and moved fifty packed boxes over to the door. I was tempted to open them to see if they were really as good as I remembered, but resisted. I could never get the covers on again if I pried them off with the pinch bar. The cellar was cold enough and damp enough. They were all right. They had to be.

At five o'clock in the morning the expressman came, and I was ready for him.

"For God's sake, be careful with these," I said. "Don't pile anything on top of them. Don't throw them onto the sidewalk. Put them anywhere they say up there, no argument. If there is any extra work, I'll make it right for you."

He grinned at me. "Don't worry," he said. "There'll be no trouble. I'm in business, too."

Three days later I picked a letter out of the mailbox. In the corner was printed PURCHASING DEPARTMENT. I hardly dared open it. It said only, "Mr. Moss asks that you call on him at your earliest convenience between ten and eleven-thirty A.M."

At quarter to ten the next morning I was once more on the bench. It was a sad day: Gray and raw, raining, and I was wet. The grass in the college yard was drenched and dun-colored. The elms dripped. I felt sick. My head ached. I trembled. My teeth chattered. What could have happened?

The door opened and Mr. Moss's secretary said, "He will see you."

Now I knew how it felt to go to the electric chair. I walked up to it, sat down, and waited for the current to be turned on.

Against the gray panes of the window I could see that Mr. Moss was smiling—getting ready to let me down easy, no doubt. I tried to smile back.

He began, "I've been making some inquiries about you. I have a friend who goes birding in your part of the country and he knows a number of people out that way. He said you were having quite a struggle."

He paused and examined his fingers. I couldn't stand it.

"The apples," I said. "Weren't they all right?"

He looked up quickly, "Sure," he said. "They were fine. Didn't you know they would be?"

I cleared my throat. "I guess so, yes. I just wondered . . ."

"They were fine," he repeated. "The order schedule is in the mail. Eight hundred boxes it came to, that's one hundred a week for eight weeks, delivered Mondays. Okay?"

"Okay," I said shakily.

"I'm sorry if I scared you," he said gently. "It was something else I wanted to talk to you about. Have a cigarette?"

I took one, trying to hide how my hand was still shaking.

"I hope you won't mind my saying that you are not much of a salesman," he remarked. "Much too thin-skinned. Not nearly enough brass. Your unusual approach interested me, more than it would some others perhaps. So I inquired around. It is just a happenstance that your father did a mastoid operation on my boy some years ago. A fine doctor and a very fine man. Of course, if the fruit had not been good, I couldn't have done anything. But it is good, it is excellent. So I think I can help you.

Pull that chair over here and I'll show you. Now how many of these Macs do you have? Fifteen hundred? That leaves seven hundred boxes to dispose of. That should be easy."

He had already typed up a half-dozen letters to purchasing agents throughout the city, addressing them by their first names.

"These three here should be good for seventy or eighty among them," he said, "and don't let this fellow off with less than ten. Now, do you have any winter apples? Greenings? Well, I don't know about those. They're good, all right, but the color puts people off. People want a red apple. I'd try to sell them at the farm or to individual customers. But Baldwins and Northern Spies, those will be fine. Of course, it's too early to start moving them now, but I'd mention them. And when you come to the end of the Macs you can push them again. The addresses are right on the envelopes; all you have to do is to mail the letters. Takes the curse off going in cold and trying to sell. That's all right, glad to do it. I owe your father a debt I can never repay."

I couldn't say a word. If I had opened my mouth I should have burst out laughing or crying, I don't know which; probably crying, for I could feel my eyes prickle, and the hall down which I almost ran was blurred as if the city fog had penetrated even there.

Of all the ordeals, of all the triumphs of those years in the orchard, this was the climax, the supreme moment. Not the cash, not the rescue from a fatal situation, but the kindness, the totally unexpected sympathy and understanding from a total stranger—ah, that was it! Wonderful, inspiring, unforgettable. I hope that when Mr. Moss and my father met under the trees of heaven, the birds were singing and the apples were ripe.

So I was rescued. Every Monday the truck carried off the apples. I continued to hold on to the small ones without fear. They were still perfect. I paid the mortgage interest, eight hundred dollars in one whack. At the bank they seemed surprised and, I thought, disappointed. They had almost had me, and I had wriggled away. Bit by bit, I began picking away at the mountain of bills. One hundred dollars here, there, and elsewhere, turn and turn about.

I lived in the kitchen and seldom went into the sunny south rooms. It would have been impossibly expensive to heat them with the worn-out old coal furnace, and wood was hard to come by. As I pruned the trees, I had carefully sawed the larger branches into logs, but they were still green. Joe and I cut and divided up the wood of an immense hickory standing barely alive in an abandoned pasture. We felt guilty as the blows of the ax rang out in the frosty air. It was a day of dead cold. The first flakes of snow hissed down on the dry leaves.

Perhaps the tree belonged to someone, and we should be arrested for stealing it. But no one came, and we cut it and sawed it and trucked it away. I kept my share for the dining room fireplace in case the family should come for Christmas. The kitchen was in an ell on the north side, dark and cheerless. There was no cellar under it and the floor was always cold. In the evenings, Freya and I huddled together on the old sofa near the stove until I gave up and went to bed in the cold cell upstairs.

The pressure was off, and I had time to think of the old man from Essex. Perhaps now that the weather had turned cold he had not been able to coax the unwilling Fred to drive. I should go and find him; I wanted to, and several times I was on the verge of starting. It would take time to hunt him up, though (why hadn't I asked his name?), and always something intervened. Then one day there was a long, thick envelope in the mailbox, addressed in brownish ink and postmarked South Essex. The letters, though wavering, were carefully shaded, and one of the *s*'s in Massachusetts had a long tail.

Dear Madam:

Perhaps you have been wondering why I have not availed myself of your kind invitation to return and revisit the house where I spent so many happy hours as a boy with my Burnham cousins. It is not for lack of desire on my part, I assure you.

I am sorry to tell you that my dear wife has been gravely ill. She was taken with a seizure shortly after our visit to your farm, and for many weeks her life was despaired of. She is now slightly better, or so the doctor professes. I myself can see but little improvement. She is pitifully weak and helpless. I have been constantly at her side, as indeed I have been for the fifty-seven years of our mar-

ried life. She seems easier when I am near, though I have had a neighbor woman in to help.

During the long night hours I have thought of the past. I told you, I believe, that the story of the Burnham family and their farm was a tragic one. I have often felt that it should be written down by one experienced in the literary art. Perhaps you know some such?

Now, thinks I, I shall write down some of these things for that kind lady who seemed so interested in an old man's story. From time to time I shall write down more as I remember and will send it to you.

In the hope that you may find the enclosed of interest,

I remain, very truly yours,

Augustus Burnham Patch

"The enclosed" was several closely written small sheets of cheap lined paper. Page one was headed "A History of the Burnham Farm," and it began:

My grandfather, Joel Burnham, was born in the year 1800, in the square farmhouse built by his grandfather in the year 1760. When I was a boy he occupied the northeast chamber and his son, my uncle Samuel, and Aunt Ruth occupied the southwest chamber overlooking the red lilac that was set out when the house was built by Joel Burnham's grandfather, Samuel. Before the building of the new house, the family had occupied the old house near the sea which was built by the first Joel Burnham in 1690. That house was struck by lightning and burned in the year 1881 or '82.

Samuel Burnham and his older brother William had been quarrelsome even as boys, my grandfather told me, and Samuel married Ruth Oakes of Salem only two days before the date set for her to marry William. It became no longer possible for them to live under the same roof. For the first time the farm was divided. Samuel was assigned the 200 acres more or less lying west of the causeway and at once set about building him a house. He was assisted in this by the neighbors as was then the custom. The teams were tied under the trees, the womenfolk prepared a collation, and there was a barrel of rum with pitchers of molasses and water for the nooning. Oak and pine for the framing of the house and barn were cut from the north woodlot and a grove was left to protect the house from the winds of winter.

The winter of 1850 was a hard one. Before Thanksgiving the ground froze and never thawed again till spring, and there were gales and heavy snow. Marshes and bays froze over solid enough to bear ox teams and pungs, and it was in this way that the quarried stone for the cellar was brought clear from West Gloucester, six miles over the ice. In February, the treacherous ice softened by the sun gave way and four span of oxen, the pung loaded with three squared blocks of granite, broke through the channel. The oxen drowned in their yokes, and Amasa Brown, attempting to cut them free, was swept under the ice and seen no more. This was all.

I sat on the fence by the mailbox, folded the sheets, and put them back in the envelope. The broad marsh stretched away, white as in that long-ago winter, glittering in the sun. Somewhere under the river ice lay the three granite blocks. Looking down from my dory as a child, I had seen them there, weed-grown and barnacled. How did they get there? I had wondered. Now I knew.

For some weeks I heard no more from Mr. Patch. Then came a short note in a hand so shaky as to be almost illegible. *"My dear wife passed away toward morning of Monday last. I am too shaken with grief to write more. . . ."* I wrote him but had no answer.

Then one day the mailman tooted, and when I ran out he placed in my hand a ragged bundle tied with mismatched bits of string.

"Too big to fit in the box," he said. "For you, though, I guess; but they weren't too sure up at the office. Kind of hard to read."

"Yes," I said, "it's for me."

I spread out the contents on the kitchen table: many sheets of the same lined paper, unnumbered, some scrawled as if by a child playing at writing, some blank. Words and paragraphs were distinguishable on a few. "Samuel dead in the woodlot his skull split, his brains run out among the leaves . . . William stood trial and after he never spoke again. Only write on paper, 'I have commit the unforgivable sin . . . put away.' They signed the paper it was to the church they thought . . . the deed to the farm and so all was lost . . ."

The last word of Mr. Patch came in the local paper: "Died in Essex, January 27, Augustus Burnham Patch, in the 86th year of his age."

The winter of '32–'33 was fine and mild. Only right before Christmas was there any cold weather. Then for a week the glass hung around ten, and the marshes and the creeks froze. A storm wild with sleet and rain brought in the black duck in thousands, and early in the morning I went out with the shotgun to see what I could do.

My older brother had done a lot of shooting, and I had gone along with my gun. I was more interested in being out on the marshes at dawn and sundown than in killing anything, so mostly I had tended the boat and set out the decoys and tramped around trying to stir the ducks out of the ditches to drive them over the blind where my brother crouched. But this year it was different; the thought of fine, rare duck meat made my mouth water. I rowed across the creek at half tide just at daybreak, and in hip boots I walked the broad marsh without decoys or blind. The first few birds that jumped up almost under my feet startled me so that I never even raised my gun, but after that I was ready and that first morning I got six fine, fat winter redlegs. I missed more than I shot, but even so six was not bad. I gave Joe three and ate a whole one for my supper that night and went to bed stuffed.

The family had said that they would be down for Christmas, and a duck dinner would be just the thing, a real treat—with applesauce, of course. But when the time came we had something better than that. On one of my trips to the marsh I heard a goose honking and spied him flying low and toward me. I squatted down in the muddy bed of a creek, and when he came into range I let him have both barrels. Down he fell in a crumple of feathers. When I picked him up I was shocked to find that he had a long string trailing from one leg: some sportsman's flying decoy. I looked nervously around but could see no one on all the wide expanse of the marshes, so I removed the string and took him home in triumph. He was fine and fat, his crop full of sportsman's corn, a real Canada goose, even if half-tame. I did not mention that at dinner, and everyone thought I was quite a hunter.

We were cheerful at Christmas. We were all together. It was a mild day and the sun streamed into the dining room. The hickory fire blazed and crackled. The house smelled deliciously of roast goose. Resolutely we did not think of past Christmases, but made the best of this one. Even my doubting brothers allowed themselves a cautious optimism when they saw the empty space in the apple cellar where the boxes had been stacked on their last visit.

"Two hundred and sixty boxes went out last Monday," I said. "Seventy-five from the sales letter: Christmas orders. All Mr. Moss's customers came through. I expect to be rid of all the packed Macs by mid-January, and the Baldwins and Spies should keep through March."

"Good enough," my older brother said.

"But what about all these small ones?" asked the younger one. "They seem pretty ripe to me." He squeezed one, and at the stem end appeared a perceptible wrinkle.

"I was offered fifty cents a box for the lot," I replied, "but I figured I would lose a dime a box at that and have been hoping for seventy anyway."

"If you keep them much longer they will be worth nothing. You had better start unloading them for anything you can get. And what about all that honey in the butler's pantry? I noticed it was starting to sugar."

"There is just no place in the house where I can keep it warm enough to prevent that unless I take it to bed with me. I have sold a little along with the apples, but honey is something that people seem to tire of very quickly. One pint per customer seems to be about the limit, and there are over fifty pints in that closet.

"Sledge sells it by the carload, but he let slip that he buys most of what he sells and improves it by adding just enough of his own to thicken it and give it flavor. He said he would take all ours; probably I shall have to let him have it, even though his price won't pay for much more than the jars. We have to have the bees, but I don't think there is any profit for us in honey."

"You had better get after those small Macs right away," my younger brother repeated as we went out the door.

The next day I called up Mr. Greenberg, and he arrived in the forenoon. It was a raw and dismal morning, overcast and drizzling. A chilly fog swirled among the trees. Mr. Greenberg obviously had a cold. He coughed and hawked in the damp cellar.

"They're pretty ripe," he complained. "And the price is low even for good stuff. Sixty is the best I can do."

"Sixty is not good enough," I said firmly. "I should lose money at that."

"I should lose at anything higher. Especially if they spoiled on me."

"Look, Mr. Greenberg, you never lose money on anything. I'm not worrying about you one bit."

"You'd be surprised at what I've lost in my life. No, you wouldn't believe me."

"Look, rather than let you have them for sixty, I'll peddle them myself. I'll just take the truck and peddle them house to house. I'd rather drive around the city hollering, 'Apples, apples, get your apples here!' than sell them to you at a loss. I could get ninety for them that way."

"You wouldn't do it, an educated woman like you, out peddling fruit."

"Yes, I would, too. What's education got to do with it?" I demanded angrily.

"If you could hear my kids talk, you'd think there were lots of things not good enough for an educated person. You think I could get my boy to sell from a pushcart like his old man did? You think my girl would spoil her hands to put them in dishwater even?"

"I don't feel that way about it at all. The only reason I wouldn't want to peddle fruit is that I wouldn't be good at it, not that I'm too good for it. But rather than give you my fruit, I will do it. You can just put that in your pipe and smoke it."

"I guess you would at that, and probably not do too bad either. You've got gall enough for anything, if you'll excuse me."

Mr. Moss had seen at once how much nerve I didn't have. It was easier to fool Mr. Greenberg, apparently. Besides, there was the case of the angry little dog in his own yard.

"Tell you what I'll do," I said, following up the advantage. "You can have the lot for seventy-five, you supply the boxes. But you get the privilege of picking them over. Anything that you think is beginning to go, pick it out. They'll keep. I've had some in the house for more than a week and they haven't wrinkled any. I wouldn't trust anybody but you in my cellar, but if you want them on these terms you can have them."

"Well, all right. I'm doing you a favor, you know it?"

"You are not," I said crossly. "I don't want any of that 'favor' stuff. Don't kid me. I know you'll make at least a quarter on every box, and that's more than I make and I grew the apples. Let's be honest and no more soft soap."

I turned my back on him and walked out into the foggy orchard to the tree where I had left my pruning saw and shears. All morning I sawed and clipped and piled the brush away from the trees to be hauled away later. I liked pruning. I liked the feeling of bending nature to my own desire to fashion a tree where the sun would touch every apple and the spray every leaf, where the picking ladders could be placed easily next fall and there were no weak branches to bear undersized fruit.

Left to itself, nature wants only to produce a great quantity of apples. A dense, brushy, twisted wild apple in a pasture shows what the trees would like to be. After two years of neglect (because my father would never allow anyone else to cut so much as a twig from one of his trees), they were going wild as fast as they could. A forest of water sprouts was shooting up from every branch. The tops were a crisscross of interlocking branches and long whips higher than the tallest ladder.

Each tree presented a new problem, and each variety had its own habit of growth that had to be considered. The Macs tended to develop weak branches that would break under a load of fruit; the Spies grew upright and brushy and tended to split in the crotches; the Baldwins tried to climb to heaven, with the best of the fruit within reach only of the angels. Naked of leaves, the Greenings had the loveliest and most characteristic shape of all. The branches began a foot or two above the ground and shot out straight from the thick, sturdy trunk with its rough gray bark. The sideways habit of growth persisted to the top and made for a low tree of immense diameter and shade so dense that it killed the grass underneath. The vigorous trees grew so thick that it was impossible to harvest the apples except from the outside. Yet I hated to cut them, so handsome were they.

All over the orchard there were huge piles of brush to show that I had not been idle, but there was still plenty left to do.

It was after noon when I went back to the cellar. I heard Mr. Greenberg coughing before I opened the door. He had about thirty boxes picked over and piled up, and there were a couple of bushels of rejects, some with small rotten spots developed around an unnoticed stem, some bruised, some withered, and a few undersized that had slipped through the grader. He had skillfully layered the good apples in the boxes, red sides up, and they looked fine, I thought. Now he was preparing to eat the lunch that he had brought in a worn imitation-leather satchel.

"For goodness' sake, you'll freeze to death out here," I said. "Come into the house where it's warm. I've got some good hot soup; it'll warm you up. And I'm going to make coffee. You can keep what's in your thermos till afternoon."

He got up from his box and came over to the door where I stood.

"You are asking me to come into your home to eat?" he said.

"Sure. I should like to have you."

"You should like to have me, she says."

"Of course I would. What's the matter, don't you want to?"

"I'm not clean to eat in a lady's house."

"You're as clean as I am, for heaven's sake. I eat in the kitchen. We can wash at the sink. Come on. Let's not stand here arguing. I'd like you to come. I get awfully sick of eating alone with a book propped up on the coffee pot."

And so he came, bringing his lunch bag and thermos. He was very quiet, and meekly washed his hands at the sink and dried them on the roller towel, then sat down at the table by the window where I had set a place for him with soup bowl, coffee cup, and spoons. He looked out at the dead brown stalks of the neglected flower garden, then around the shabby kitchen. His one good eye took in everything: the shabby sofa near the stove, the half-empty cupboard above the sink, the worn linoleum with the rat hole in the corner.

"I said you'd be surprised at what I've lost in my life. Perhaps you wouldn't," he said suddenly, out of a clear sky.

"I'm beyond being surprised at anything," I said, setting a bowl of soup in front of him and sitting down in my place. "But not beyond being interested. What did you mean? What have you lost?"

"When I said it, I was thinking of money. We were talking about money, remember? But working over the apples this morning I got thinking. Perhaps I've lost more than money—hope, maybe, or a reason for going on. Now, for you it seems different: Money you have lost, I see. But hope, no."

"To me you seem to be pretty well fixed," I observed. "Your own business, your own truck."

"But for what? That's what I ask myself. I was a little boy when we came from Russia. In the old country my father was an educated man, a rabbi. When he died my mother took the children and came to her brother in New York. Here in the Promised Land there would be education. But it was not so. For me there was only work. For her, work—till it killed her. For my brothers, for my sister, work. At first it seemed to me not so good as at home. But here there was no ghetto, no pogroms, and by and by I could see that for Americans there was something. Good, so I would be an American. And my children, they would be educated. Well, they are—and still I wonder."

"Why?" I asked.

"I will tell you. To me education is everything. I had enough while my father was living, till I was ten years old, to see it was everything. But then I had to go to work. I saved my money and bought a pushcart, then saved and bought another. My uncle had that and paid me a percentage. Then I bought a truck, old. Then a truck, new. Then a tenement house, on credit. Then, more credit: an apartment house. Then the crash.

No more apartment house, tenement, truck, business. Only the pushcart. Boston, this time, not New York. Now I am back to the truck and the little business. Maybe next year the tenement. And so on. And for what?"

"For your children, I suppose," I said, "to give them what you have missed. Isn't that reason enough?"

"I always thought so. That's why I went on. And now I have money to send my boy to college, to medical school, law school. And what does he want? To hang around street corners. Such a cheap crowd, you should see. To play in a jazz band, in the nightclubs. 'All right,' I said, 'you want music. You should go to the conservatory, then.' Oh, no—not that kind of music. The great music of the world is not for my boy. 'This is America, Poppa, none of that old-country stuff.' The girl, just the same: wild, fresh to her mother. 'Bring your boyfriend home.' 'Oh no, Momma, he's an American. He wouldn't like it here.' Ashamed of us. The fruit peddler. The old Jewish woman with not so good English."

"I have never heard anything so terrible," I burst out.

" 'Terrible,' no. Sad, tragic, maybe. What have I done wrong? It must be because I am not educated."

"Oh, no, it isn't that. I'm sure it isn't that. They are the ones who are not educated. Not you."

"But they have been to school."

"Just the same, they are not educated."

He shook his head sadly.

I filled his soup bowl and coffee cup again. How little we can do for a suffering human being. My father could ease the suffering of the body. Here Mr. Greenberg sat and suffered in my kitchen, and all I could do was give him a bowl of soup.

At last he said, "You could do something for me, if you would. You could talk to my children. You could come into my house, to show them that a real American lady is not ashamed to eat with us. I will invite you—will you come?"

"Of course I will, Mr. Greenberg," I said. "Any time you say. But I think that your children wouldn't see much sense in what I am doing, either. To them it would look foolish, anyone struggling and slaving to hang on to a place to keep a family together. But I can honestly say to them that I greatly admire their father, for all that he has done for them and for what he stands for. That I would be happy to do." I thought to myself that I'd like to knock their empty heads together. Poor Mr. Greenberg cried, and I almost did, too.

There was nothing emotional about the Greenberg children. They were a hard-eyed, handsome pair. I had tried for Mr. Greenberg's sake to get myself up as close as possible to an "American lady," but in the face of Esther Greenberg, aged seventeen, I felt that I had failed. It was not that she was not polite—she was, very. But I was painfully aware that hard work with the tractor had widened my shoulders so that the gabardine suit jacket strained at the seams. Knots of muscle stood out under the silk stockings that had one small run on the inside. My hands, over which I had worked hard, still looked coarse and red by contrast with Esther's, which were tapering, smooth, and white as a nail-polish advertisement. Young Sam, older by a year or two than his sister, shook hands limply and said "Howdydo" when introduced, then went back to his chair where he sat silently, examining his fingers.

Mr. Greenberg, dressed to the nines in a blue serge suit, stiff collar, and bright red tie, fluttered about: pulling up a chair for me near the floor lamp with its beaded fringe, then moving the lamp away, then bringing a little table with cigarettes and a souvenir ashtray, then scuttling to the kitchen after matches, and finally lighting my cigarette with such solicitude that he almost singed my eyelashes.

There was nothing awkward about Mrs. Greenberg, although she spoke very little English. She was running back and forth between the kitchen and table, which was set in the alcove; each time she went by, accompanied by a fine smell of roasting chicken, she beamed at me and patted me on the shoulder. She was fat and had probably had as much trouble getting into her purple crepe dress as I had had with my suit. Her broad forehead was beaded with perspiration and her gray hair beginning to straggle, but in the flat Slavic face her blue eyes were bright and kind. The children evidently got their dark looks from their father's side.

I could think of no way to put myself or anyone else at ease. Mr. Greenberg and I talked in a desultory way about the apple business.

"She is a farmer, a lady farmer. She works—harder than a man, even," Mr. Greenberg explained. "Only in America would you find such a thing, a college girl who feels not too proud to work in the fields like a man—"

"Oh, Poppa," Esther said, embarrassed, "no one wants to hear about the old country."

"You're wrong there," I said quickly. "That's all America is, a new place made up from all the old countries everywhere. The bad things of the old countries have been left behind there, but new Americans like your father have brought the good things of Europe with them. If a country is made up of all the good things from everywhere, it should be the best in the world." I had not meant to preach, but I blundered on. "My great-grandfather came from France. Your father came from Russia. Two of the men who picked apples with me this fall were Polish Americans, and the third a Frenchman. It is the combination of all these things that makes this country a wonderful place—that is, if we understand and appreciate the background that lies so close to all of us."

Esther's face was expressionless, but Sam looked up with a flicker of interest.

"Take music, for instance," I said, glancing toward the piano, with its sheets of popular music spread on the rack, and the saxophone in its case leaning beside it. "So far America has produced jazz, with its African accent. Jazz can express something that is in us, but not all—nowhere near all. So many voices need to join in."

"I don't get you," Sam said suddenly.

"I don't wonder. I live so much alone and talk so little that my words are rusty. I find them hard to pull out when I want them. But there's music to be written—."

"Now I get you all right. You sound just like Poppa: America is just work, work, and more work. I don't want to write music—make arrangements for the band, okay, but I do that now. If I went to the conservatory like Poppa says, would it help me to get a job as first sax, with Paul Whiteman, say?"

"Probably it wouldn't; I don't know."

"Well, what's the point of it, then? Can I help it if Grandpa was a rabbi back in Russia? I just want to go to New York and play in a name band—Samuel Green, first sax with Paul Whiteman: Green, not Greenberg." He glanced quickly at his father.

Mr. Greenberg opened his mouth to say something, then closed it again and shook his head.

"I never saw anybody on the society pages named Greenberg," Esther said defiantly.

At this moment, much to my relief, Mrs. Greenberg called us to supper. As I ate roast chicken, peas, potatoes, gravy, and black bread with sweet butter, I felt that I was doing so under false pretenses. I could not help this situation, unless by enjoying the food, perhaps. And I did do that.

On the long road home in the truck I thought over the evening, and many times afterward out among the trees. I was sorry for the Greenberg children, under impossible pressure between the old world and the new, and terribly sorry for Mr. Greenberg, who felt that all his efforts had come to nothing. They all could learn something from Mrs. Greenberg, I thought, who put no pressure on anyone except to take a second helping of chicken and gravy.

I made up my mind that the next time I saw Mr. Greenberg I wouldn't raise any big issues. There had been too much dynamite already. So I just said, "I had a good time, and a wonderful feast. I liked the kids a lot. They are just young, that's all, and having a hard time living up to what you expect of them. I think in time you'll find your efforts have not been wasted. No effort ever is wasted, I'm sure of that."

We never mentioned the subject again. But though we haggled and bickered over the apples, we were friends always.

By the first week in April the cellar was empty, and my hopes grew higher with the sun. It had been a good winter with hardly any snow; January was so mild that I had been able to work outdoors in shirtsleeves. All the bills were paid, and when the last of the cash came in there would be two thousand dollars to start the year. The trees were all pruned, and as soon as the high ground was dry enough I began hauling away the brush, piling it along the edge of the marsh for burning next winter. Hope and optimism were at high tide.

But even in the moment of exultation, my spirits would suddenly shift and change as unaccountably as the April day that, starting sunny and warm, by noon would be foggy and dark under the breath of the east wind. Last year in the face of failure and ruin I had not felt so. How ironic that the first bit of success should be accompanied by the chill of foreboding. At first I tried to drown the mood in work, good old work, but I had to stop when it grew dark, and sitting on the sofa after supper I could feel the fog move in again, chilling my spirits as outside it pressed against the window and blotted out the stars.

"What is it, Freya?" I said to the dog. "What is wrong with me?" And suddenly I knew what it was. The farm could be made to pay, of that I was sure. But to do it I should have to be alone. Too big for one, too small for two. Suddenly, when I spoke the words out loud, everything was clear—a whole succession of years, alone. And that was not for me. I jumped up off the sofa and walked restlessly about. Freya watched me with her sad eyes, her forehead wrinkled with worry. Looking at her I had to laugh, and then abruptly I felt better.

"Don't worry, good old dog. It's all right. I'll think of something." I had said the words and faced the fact: everything was in the clear. By next winter, I should have to think of something.

Two thousand dollars with the mortgage interest paid through July sounded like plenty of money, but after some figuring with a carpenter's pencil out in the barn it did not look so wonderful after all. April through September was six months; the only income in all that time would be from the peaches. I dared not hope they would do as well as last season. Peaches produce only on the new wood of the previous year, and the trick with them is to keep them always growing. When the old wood is cut back they send out whips with dark red bark, and on these the triple buds for next year's fruit form and develop.

The trees had not been pruned for several years, and their new growth was limited to the tips of long, weak branches. They were pretty that way, but not profitable. Looking to the future, I had to be drastic with them. The oldest trees I cut back almost to the trunk; the strongest lost two thirds of their wood, new and old. They looked pathetic, and I had qualms when I saw the piles of brush tipped with triple buds, this year's crop, to be hauled away and burned. But it was the thing to do. With luck, mulching, and heavy feeding they should grow three or four feet of strong new wood, and in later years light pruning should keep them under control.

And of course there would be expenses. I should have to buy boxes this year. Even if I bought shooks and made them up in my spare time, the boxes would come to two hundred dollars. Spray materials would be around four hundred dollars; gasoline, another hundred; food and living expenses I would struggle to keep to two hundred. Half my total capital was right there, and nothing allowed for labor. Fading was the hope of having Joe full-time. To achieve that I should have to take Charlie's advice and set out intermediate crops. I took the plunge and ordered one thousand asparagus roots and five hundred raspberries. This again was long-range planning. It would be three years before I could cut the asparagus in any amount, and the raspberries would not produce until next year.

Looking to the future was part of the fascination of farming. And looking to the past. I felt that I was swimming in a river with a deep, irresistible current, a force that stemmed from some running spring far back in the hills behind me and that swept me ever onward into an unknown future. I could not change the flow or direction of the current. I could only alter my own course to take advantage of it, to avoid whirlpools and backwaters so that I moved smoothly with it. The seasons changed with immutable rhythm, and each one found me still swimming midstream. It was a wonderful feeling of security and certainty in a world neither safe nor sure.

There was a strip of fine black earth, an acre or more that ran down through the middle of the peach orchard where there were no trees, and here I decided to set out the asparagus bed. Years before my grandmother's asparagus had flourished here, and I remembered going out with her as a child carrying the basket and oddly shaped knife; the rows were marked by the brown stalks of last year's crop, and I dashed up and down searching out the first fat green shoots while the black dog Nixie capered and barked and the birds sang. Sometimes I would be allowed to cut a sprout, carefully, just below the ground, avoiding the pale shoots pushing up through the darkness to find the sun.

But now I hitched the two-wheeled plough to the tractor and turned under the self-sown buckwheat that had conveniently killed out the grass. My father must have had plans for that bit of land. He had planted buckwheat there two years before, and though it had never been turned under, it had reseeded itself and had grown each summer more thick and lush. The insignificant pinkish flowers had furnished the bees with plenty of dark, bitter honey for their winter stores. This year the roots and young leaves would furnish humus for the new crop.

I still had to add manure, and I bought four loads from a whiskered friend of old Louis, who obligingly dumped the steaming piles in strategic places to be spread by hand and harrowed in. He looked critically at my ploughing job: the furrows were not quite straight and were of uneven depth here and there, but he said nothing. I thought it looked very fine for a first attempt, and I had loved doing it, watching the ribbon of black unrolling behind the bright ploughshare and sniffing the fine spring smell of freshly turned loam. As I spread the manure with the six-tined fork, the rich scent recalled with painful vividness the old days when the cows sighed comfortably in their stanchions, the horses stamped in the stalls, and there was no machinery. I should have liked that kind of farming best.

The asparagus plants were queer-looking things, a web of pale roots like something from the bottom of the sea. From the crown of each sprouted a few pallid, feeble shoots that I hoped time and the fertile loam would encourage to grow stout and green. I set out the raspberry canes in a spot of lighter loam and then, all in a rush, it was time for the oil spray for scale, the one that I had missed last year.

I had not seen Joe for several weeks. The Wildcats had been on tour, playing almost every night in the surrounding towns. His older brother Bernie had got a job driving a truck for the state, and the LaPlante fortunes were looking up. Everyone was having breakfast, Joe had said with a grin. If he was disappointed when I told him how I was fixed, he did not show it.

"Three days a week will work out fine for me," he said, cheerfully. "Kip comes from Newburyport, you know, and he thinks he can get us plenty engagements playing at the beaches and at the Dance Hall next summer. Five bucks a night apiece, he thinks. We're getting four now. We've done good all winter and what with Bernie's job, my mother hasn't had to go to the

Town Hall for a long time. She's been working herself, down at the hotel, making beds and cleaning up. One buck for four hours, can you imagine? But I guess business is not good there. Probably they couldn't do better."

What a difference it made, spraying with two instead of one. We took turns: I drove in the morning and sprayed in the afternoon. We moved up and down between the rows with the tractor hauling the heavy hose instead of our having to manhandle it through the grass and around the trees. Not that we didn't have our troubles, but they were not half so bad when shared with curses or laughter.

Unfortunately Joe was no better a mechanic than I. Neither of us could ever fathom why the tractor engine died or the spray engine quit when they had been running perfectly. It always happened at the most inopportune moment, in the steepest part of the orchard, at the devil's curve above the pumphouse, or when we were rushing to finish before a rising breeze picked up too much strength. Our remedy was to crank and crank until the balky thing started. A mechanic would have adjusted something—but what, we never knew.

There was the day when, starting out with a fresh tank from the fill pipe, the nozzle clogged almost at once and only a drizzle ran out over my hands and up my arm. Joe released the pressure and I unscrewed the cap, picked out the particles, and screwed it back on. Five minutes later the same thing happened. And yet again. It was infuriating.

There were only two choices: pull the plug and empty fifteen dollars' worth of spray on the ground, or continue as best we could until what spray had not soaked me was on the trees and the tank was empty. Joe insisted on changing places with me and finally, exhausted and furious, I let him. His dark skin did not burn as readily as mine, but when at last the tank was drained we were both well blistered. In disgusted silence we drove back to the barn. There Joe climbed up on top of the tank, lifted the square hatch cover, and peered in.

"Oh, oh," he said. "I see what it is. The strainer's off."

I took his place and looked in. I could see the suction hose that ran from the pump to within a couple of inches of the bottom of the tank. Beneath it, awash in the residue, lay the brass-wire strainer. A simple thing to fix. Stick it back on the hose and wire it with a new piece of copper wire, of which there was a spool in the tool room. I fetched a length of it and a pair of pliers while Joe unscrewed the drain plug on the bottom of the tank. I handed the things up to him and sat down in the shade. I could see his short legs scrabbling for a foothold, and there was a muffled curse from inside the tank.

"What's the matter?" I asked.

"By Gar, I can't reach it. For what did they make this thing? A dwarf? I can't get my shoulders through and my arms are way too short."

"Let me try," I said. "I'm thinner than you and my arms are longer."

"You'll need a light. When you plug up the hole it's dark in there." So we got a flashlight and I climbed up. I could not reach the strainer either.

"Hold on to my feet," I directed Joe. "If I can get my shoulders through the hatch, I might be able to get it. What a crazy way to make anything, so small."

Scrambling and squirming I worked my shoulders through. I could reach the hose, but hanging head down and almost cut in two by the sharp edge of the hatchway, I couldn't do anything. The flashlight gave a feeble light.

"Let go of my feet," I directed, and before he had time to stop me, I had hitched and wriggled through the opening and was crouching inside the tank.

Joe's anxious face appeared in the hatchway. "This is fine," I said reassuringly. "Just get out of the light and I'll have it fixed in a minute."

"But can you get out again?"

"Sure," I said confidently. "If I got in, I should be able to get out."

The tank was slippery and smelled strongly of sulphur. I had to squat cross-legged, folded up like a carpenter's ruler, as I forced the strainer onto the hose and wired it, twisting the soft copper tight with the pliers.

"There," I said at last. "That will never come off. Now to get out of here."

And that, it turned out, was not so easy. In the cramped quarters I could not maneuver into the right position to force my shoulders through the narrow opening. Again and again my feet and knees slipped on the slimy wood. Joe grabbed my wrists and tried to haul me out, but I could not work my shoulders through. At last we gave up and I squatted down again, bruised and breathless.

"You'll have to saw me out," I panted. "Get the cross-cut and put a new blade in the hacksaw. It's going to be tough. The wood is wet and you'll have to cut through one of the Carlings. For God's sake hurry up, before I pass out in here."

I heard him run off toward the barn. He seemed gone forever as I crouched there, resisting with difficulty the impulse to scream and struggle. It took nearly two hours to cut the hatch, and when it was done, I was too cramped to move and had to be hauled out. I saw a man fall overboard from a fishing boat one day, rubber boots, oilskins, and all. He grabbed the trawl wires and we had him back aboard in a minute, but he was no good the rest of the day, just lay in his bunk. I sprawled under a tree, not caring whether we ever got the spraying done, while Joe enlarged the cover to fit the hatch.

Somehow we worked through the spray schedule. The oil sprayer and the tractor stuck in the mud of the flat ground. That early spring the wind blew during part of every one of Joe's working days, so I had to finish the work alone, and just in time. The electric pump on the well quit, worn out at last.

Then the welcome interlude while the trees blossomed. For ten days the bees were supposed to do their stuff, ten anxious days when the fruit grower prays for warm, bright weather, dreads a frost at night, and curses a spell of fog or rain. The trees did not blossom as heavily as last year. The Baldwins were resting and their rows ran like a dark ribbon through the shell-pink snowdrift of McIntosh. With good weather and perhaps a better price, we should be all right. The weather was perfect, sunny and windless. The bees boomed and cavorted among the blossoms, and everything looked fine for a heavy set.

There was no time to enjoy the beauty of the season. A peach spray had to be put on—a gentle mixture of wettable sulphur and arsenate of lead. Bouquets of Greening and Russet blossoms had to be hung in every other tree in the young block of five hundred Macs for cross-pollination, and they needed to be replaced when withered. Worst of all, I had to buy a new pump and motor for the well, two hundred dollars on which I had not figured.

Water supply had always been a problem on the glacial drumlin that was the farm. As far as we could discover, there had been no well in colonial times, and the family depended on the rainwater collected in two immense, bottle-shaped brick cisterns beside the house. They were fed by a complicated system of gutters and rain spouts that looked like a map of the Mississippi and its tributaries, draining every square inch of the roof. With modern plumbing and washing habits the cisterns became inadequate and always went dry in times of drought.

My father thought a dowsing rod unscientific and hired an engineering firm to find us a well. At huge expense they drove pipes in all the likely-looking places—without result. Finally they struck a gusher, and there the well was driven and the pumphouse built. Unfortunately it was one thousand feet from the house and two hundred feet from the road where, eventually, the power lines would run. But the water was sweet and good, so a pipeline was sunk, five feet deep, all the way to a tank on the hilltop whence it fed by gravity into the house. A gasoline engine gasped and shivered in the pumphouse to supply the power.

The supply was inexhaustible: a subterranean river, so the engineers said. My father generously donated free water to three or four neighbors with water trouble, and day and night the engine coughed without stopping to keep first one and then two storage tanks full. After some months of this we began to notice a queer taste in the water and an undissolved soapy scum in the bathtub, but we couldn't admit it to ourselves until the neighbors began to complain. The engineers were summoned and shrugged their shoulders.

"By drawing so heavily on the supply you have broken through the freshwater vein into the underlying brackish vein," they said. "No, there's nothing to do about it. Possibly it might clear itself." But it never did.

One by one the neighbors found good wells of their own, but they were careful not to make the same mistake we had. For years we got along with the most complicated plumbing ever imagined: cistern water in the laundry, hot and cold, and in the hot water pipes all over the house, with valves to turn on the well water in case the cistern ran dry. There were pipes everywhere: underground, in the partitions, and a regular spiderweb on the kitchen ceiling. There was an abandoned storage tank in the attic into which I once let the water by turning the wrong valve in the laundry. A hundred gallons had collected in it before I found out why it had been given up—it leaked. About fifty gallons poured down through two ceilings, and the rest I bailed with a bucket and threw out the attic skylight. The place was a plumber's dream.

(Years later, when my husband's and my return to the place depended on our finding a water supply for the little house behind the barn where I had spent my orchard summers, we retained a water dowser from a neighboring town. He walked out back of the house with his forked stick, stamped his heel into the spot where the pull was strongest, and drove a fine well not fifty feet from a dry pipe that marked one of the failures of the engineers. It did happen to be contaminated; but the dowser was not supposed to know that, and neither did we until after we left, as healthy and happy as when we came.)

Water trouble made the summer rental of the farmhouse difficult, yet we counted on this to pay the heavy taxes and insurance. It would be too good luck to have again our wonderful tenants of the year before, and sure enough, in midwinter a letter had come from Miss Rosamond saying with real regret that they had decided to visit their nieces in the mountains this year. My younger brother, the supersalesman, got busy; but in 1933 the people who could afford to rent summer houses were even more frightened by the New Deal than they had been by the old one.

On every fine weekend of the spring, I watched hopefully for a strange car to turn in the farmhouse driveway. The weekend when the hawthorn tree hid the weathered shingles in a snowdrift of blossoms—no one could have resisted it then. Or the days when the pyrus shrubs blazed, scarlet and salmon-pink; or the lilacs, the high hedges of lavender and white, or the ancient, wine-red tree in front of the house. All these bloomed and faded, and no one came.

The house was still empty when the great English linden flowered from top to bottom early in July. I was standing in its shade, half drunk with the perfume and listening to the bees rumbling among the millions of pale, waxy blossoms, when I was aware of a car stopping by the front door. Slowly, not too eagerly, I went toward it and saw to my dismay that it was the man from the bank. What did he want, now that the interest was paid? I soon found out.

"House not rented this year?"

"No," I answered, "not yet."

"Well," he said, "if you don't mind my saying so, I can see why. This is a bad year for seashore real estate. Only places in top-notch condition are fetching what they should, and the directors feel that this property is not in top-notch condition. Far from it."

"What's wrong with it?" I said hotly. "We put on the new roof, and the orchard—"

"I see the roof, yes, that was a must, wasn't it? As to the orchard, our bank is not interested in agricultural mortgages. We consider them much too risky for our stockholders. We are concerned with residential properties, and if the bank were to take this property over, we should divide it into house lots and recover our investment in that way."

"But how could you take it over? The interest is paid, has always been paid, right on time or in advance."

"Perhaps you did not realize that the terms of the mortgage require an annual payment on the principal of one thousand dollars. This payment is two years in arrears. The bank would be quite justified in foreclosing at any time."

Suddenly I could see his game: cat and mouse. The cat was happy to play with the mouse for a while, letting her run a little and gently bringing her back. He would pounce when the time was right. But the mouse had one more trick up her sleeve.

"I will send you my check for one thousand dollars tomorrow morning," I said calmly. "I should hardly think the bank would foreclose in the face of my obvious intent to pay. I thought the interest payment included something on the principal, or I should have taken care of it before. It was never explained to me."

"An oversight," he assured me. "I agree that probably the bank will postpone foreclosure proceedings, in consideration of a partial payment on the principal. Now, if I may make the suggestion, two or three coats of paint would dress up the house a great deal."

"I won't do it," I said defiantly. "We like the weathered clapboards the way they've always been."

He did not insist, just shrugged his shoulders and started the engine of his Cadillac.

I sent him the check. That was the end of my stake, the last of the yawl money.

In midmonth my brother turned up a tenant, a nervous, recently divorced lady with two spoiled children and an irascible cook. I hauled ten gallons of drinking water from a neighbor's twice a day and did everything else I could to please them, but they were never satisfied. Their rent was less than half that of the previous year's tenants; we were lucky to get even that. There would be a seven-hundred-dollar deficit on the taxes and insurance.

If anyone had tapped me on the shoulder and said, "And *now* what are you going to do?" I should have answered quite confidently, "I don't know, but it will be all right. We will hang on to it." My worries were not more serious than the bites of insects in the orchard on muggy days, and there always came a breeze to blow them away. Good old work could dispel them— that, and the satisfaction of watching the peach trees put forth long, red-barked shoots on which the triple buds were already forming, of seeing the apple trees shapely and neat after their pruning job, with big, vigorous leaves and fruits well set, already turning fuzzy pink cheeks to the sun.

Occasionally I wished that I only had to concern myself with producing the fruit and tilling the soil, free of the crushing pressures of time and money. As I swung the scythe or turned the handle of the honey extractor, I used to dream of diking some of the marsh, letting it freshen with the rain, and growing cranberries; or of converting an abandoned gravel pit into a freshwater pond and raising giant bullfrogs for the frogs' legs market. I read every word of the leaflets that I found in the mailbox addressed only to RFD Boxholder and had great fun with the agricultural dreams they evoked. The only trouble was that I had to keep both my worries and my dreams to myself. Everyone in the family was struggling hard, each in his or her own sphere—but were I to fail, the others would be dragged down, too. My brothers had made that clear enough. So I kept quiet and hoped for the best.

Before I knew it the tenants' time was up, and without regret I watched them depart. Almost before they were out of sight, I popped back into my winter quarters in the kitchen and it was time for the harvest.

We began on the eighth of September, Kasimir, Stanley, Joe, and I. Old Louis had been sick all summer, and Carl had gone fishing. With the trees pruned and the Baldwins resting I figured that the four of us could handle the crop. Also, I was very short of cash, as I had taken in only one hundred fifty dollars from the peaches. The trees looked splendid: reborn again and loaded with buds for next year.

From the beginning this autumn of 1933 was different from the last, at first in subtle ways hard to define. There were no languid hazy days; instead, bright, hard blue skies and stiff northwesters or sullen easterlies and the sea growling on the sandbars at night. Every clear morning the grass was crisp with frost. The leaves blazed and the marshes were golden a good six weeks before their time. Like an animal, nervous and restless before an impending storm, I felt in my bones something brewing in the sea of air around us.

Last year we had begun with the big Mac trees in the oldest orchard, then moved across the road and to the small block east of the house. Last of all we had picked the young trees in the north block, waiting till they came to the fullest perfection of color.

This year, too, they were the best: none smaller than 2¾ inches, and the trees were loaded. Playing a hunch, we began in the north, working fast up and down the long rows, beginning with the most exposed trees edging the marsh. The first load looked greener in the boxes than they had on the trees, and for a moment I had doubts, but driven by my feeling of foreboding, we continued. Joe and I had cleared out the barn to make more space, and we packed every inch full before we began grading out. Every minute spent in the barn I was uneasy, and every noon I tapped the barometer beside the kitchen sink. Day after day it held steady, and the northwest wind blew persistent, but without strength to shake the apples down.

On the seventeenth, we had nine hundred boxes packed and fifty trees to go. There were enough apples to fill four hundred boxes in the barn, so we should have to pack tomorrow. The northwester had died out, and it had been a day of absolute calm and very warm. By midafternoon a smoky veil of cloud began to dim the sun; it did not set, just disappeared as the cloud veil thickened. At four o'clock I went into the kitchen and tapped the barometer. It had dropped a tenth.

Back at the barn I said, "How would you boys feel about picking tonight as long as we can see and beginning tomorrow morning before daybreak? I don't like the looks of the weather at all."

"Okay," Joe said, "but where are you going to put them?"

"We can leave them in picking boxes under the trees. There'll be no sun to spoil them, I think, and it won't hurt them to get wet."

"What about the rest of them? The big trees?"

"It's too late to do anything about them now. If it blows from the northwest the windbreak should protect them some. That's what it was planted for; let's hope it's big enough to do its stuff."

The murky night shut down early, but we had ten trees clean before we had to quit. It was pitch-dark and starless when I picked the men up in town in the morning.

"No wind yet," Joe observed.

"There is, though—just a breath from the northeast. You can't feel it here. The sea was very loud all night."

"Did you hear the radio?" Stanley asked. "Said there was a big storm coming up the coast. Tail of a hurricane, the man called it."

"I heard it," I said. "They hoped it might go to sea south of Nantucket, but I don't think so. The bottom has fallen out of the barometer since last evening."

When I shut the truck off in the barnyard the roar of the sea took over where the engine noise left off, a thundering rumble uncanny in the warm and windless dark.

"Boy," Joe said. "I never heard it as loud as that, even in winter."

"Could we see to pick yet, do you suppose?" Kasimir asked nervously.

"I doubt it, but we might as well get down there," I said.

By the time we got the tractor started and the trailer loaded with boxes and hitched, there was a little gray light from nowhere. The apples showed as black blobs among the paler leaves, and we began, working fast and in silence. An occasional gust moaned through the tops of the trees and died away. The air was of a tropic warmth, salty and wet.

As daylight imperceptibly increased we could see the sky, a slate-gray wrack broken by mares' tails. The first clouds of the storm itself were driving in low from the sea, moving fast on a wind that as yet we could not feel. At nine o'clock there was a spatter of rain, driven by a hard gust that shook the trees. A few apples fell thumping down. There were fifteen trees to go. At ten-thirty the wind was so stiff that it was hard to balance on the stepladders. In the shrieking gusts we had to hang on with both hands, while the fruit rained down from the writhing branches. Then the rain came, a rush of warm drops that for a moment killed the wind.

"Okay," I said. "That does it." There were five to go.

"Hell," said Joe. "Let's not quit now. Let's finish. What do you say?"

"Sure," said the others, both together.

"You'll get soaked," I protested.

"Couldn't be much wetter," Stanley said cheerfully as he climbed down his ladder with a full bag. His fair hair was plastered to his head, and the water streamed down his face. His shoes squelched as he walked.

At a quarter past eleven we had them all—all that the wind had not gathered. Upward of two hundred boxes were ranged under the trees.

"Five hundred bucks, this morning's work has saved me," I said. "Thanks!"

"Tell you what we'll do, if it's all right with you," Joe said after consulting with the others. "I'll take us up in the truck, and we'll put on something dry and eat and be back at one o'clock to get after the ones in the barn."

"That would be swell," I said. "And on your way back, pick up some beer. It would taste about right around four o'clock, don't you think?" I handed him a soaked wad of bills from my dungarees pocket.

After they had gone I squelched out to the block of big trees to see how they were doing. I would not have been surprised to find half the apples on the ground. Miraculously, the mane of spruces along the crest of the hill was sheltering them so that even the topmost branches hardly moved. A shift of the wind to the southerly would be bad, but there was no sign of that. The clouds were driving straight from the northeast, almost brushing the tops of the tossing evergreens. Across the road the trees were sheltered by the hill. The east block was dropping badly, but there were not many trees there. I wondered how they were doing on the flat acres and easterly slopes of Goodale Orchard.

After dinner I called them up. The manager answered.

"I would say one third are down already," he said gloomily. "A wind shift to the north tonight like the radio says should bring off a lot more. How are yours?"

"The windbreak is saving us so far. And a shift to the north would be all right, too."

"How about your north block? Losing many there?"

"None," I replied. "We picked the last of them before noon."

"You're lucky," he said sourly. "Your guys work this morning, did they?"

"Sure. We began at daybreak and worked right up to eleven-thirty. Kind of wet, the last of it."

"Mine quit before ten and came back to the barn. Guess we'll do mostly picking up drops from now on. The market should be loaded with them if this storm hits very far inland."

"I'm sorry. It's tough luck," I said sympathetically. But I could not help feeling that his chickens were coming home to roost.

All afternoon we ran the bright fruit through the grader while the wind roared in the trees and the rain lashed the shingles. At four o'clock we drank our beer, easy and friendly together. With the grader shut off we could hear the old barn creaking and groaning as the pegged timbers of the frame worked under the shocks of the blasts. But it was built like a ship, made to give to the sea, and it stood foursquare. The hand-hewn timbers of the stoutly braced roof were as sound as the day the Burnhams and their neighbors had raised them, almost two hundred years before.

In the night I was wakened by a new sound of the wind in the large branches outside the window. From my bed I could see stars in the small, square panes. The wind was in the north and it had blown clear. I went back to sleep, content.

Before we had the grader started the next morning, Mr. Greenberg appeared. His truck was piled high with empties, and he had two helpers with him.

"I thought if I got here early," he said, "I could get a load of your drops into market ahead of the rush and get a little better price, maybe. When we heard the wind I said to the wife, 'That poor lady down there, all her fruit on the ground.' Well, if it's right with you we'll get busy picking them up. Mac drops tomorrow will be worth nothing."

"You'll find less than a hundred bushels on the whole place," I said triumphantly. "We got the young orchard picked ahead of the storm, thanks to the boys here, and the windbreak on the hill sheltered the others."

"That's good, that's wonderful!" Mr. Greenberg said heartily. "I am glad for you that you should be lucky. I will take, then, what you have and finish at Goodale's. I guess there will be plenty there to keep us hauling right along. I can't quote you a price till I see what's come in. Yesterday, thirty-five; today, maybe a quarter; tomorrow, a dime, a nickel, I don't know. Should I take them so? Will you trust me?"

"Of course. Do the best you can. You'll find most of them in the east block and the rest in the jog in the young orchard. That was where we ended up."

There were ninety-three boxes, for which he got me twenty cents each. Within a couple of days they were down to a nickel, and no takers.

"Hold your good stuff," Mr. Greenberg said when he paid me. "By Thanksgiving the market should be good."

The storm cleared the air for days afterward, but the wind had stripped off many of the bright leaves. The weather, too, remained unseasonably cold. It looked and felt like winter. We worked all day in sweaters and jackets, galoshes and wool socks. The sun seemed to have lost its power too soon. The barn was like an icebox, and there was no problem keeping the storage cellar chilled. My cold fingers slipped on the wrapping papers, and I had to keep them sticky with apple juice to maintain speed. At full steam I could pack one hundred fifty bushels in a nine-hour day, but probably I averaged less. At any rate, with this year's crop running large and clean, thanks to the pruning, I couldn't keep up.

Joe had been dying to try packing, so we set up a stand at the 3-inch bin for him. He caught on at once, and before many days I had to stay on my toes to keep ahead of him. With two packing, Stanley and Kassie had to keep moving, too. They stood on either side of the sorting table until the 2¼–2½-inch bins filled; then they would take turns running to bundle them into boxes. When our bins piled up they shut the grader off and topped the boxes on the press until we caught up. Then the rumbling and rhythmic swish and rustle of the papers began again.

Fruit packing is done in fast waltz time, *one* two three, *one* two three. Probably that's why Joe was so good at it. On the count of one, the left hand picks an apple from the bin and the right swishes a paper from the tray where the stack is held by a needle and a spring. It takes skill to slide just one paper out without disarranging the stack. Count two tosses the apple from the left hand into the center of the paper in the right; and three, in one complicated descending motion, wraps the apple and tucks it into its place, paper skirt down, with a twist of the wrist.

For smooth speed, the hands have to work in rhythm, freewheeling, independent of the mind. Concentration on any one motion breaks the spell. The hand fumbles and slips among the papers; the fruit misses the center of the wrapper, rolls on the floor, or bruises against the side of the box. Soothed by the rumble of the grader and stimulated by the recurring rhythmic motion, my mind worked along in parallel, skipping between the past and the future. I remembered poetry I had forgotten, people I had known, and places I had been. Deliberately I focused on a scene or a person, recalling for my own amusement and contemplating with the closest attention every minuscule detail, while the hours passed, *one* two three, *one* two three.

Long afterward this training stood me in good stead. I worked three years on the assembly line of a factory, and I was neither worn out nor bored. Despite the lapse of time, I slipped right into the rhythm of the moving belt, feeling in my bones when it would slide forward. Each series of motions was identical, fitted into a few seconds like matched pieces of a puzzle into a frame. Only when the mechanism did not operate properly—when the belt got out of time, when the screw holes were a fraction out of line or the electric drill did not start up smoothly—was there such a frustration as to leave me exhausted at day's end.

But I doubt that the free time for the mind gained on such rhythmic manual operations could ever be used for really creative effort. I do not think that anyone ever will compose a symphony or a novel or a fresco design while geared to the moving belt in a factory. The closest I ever came to any original thinking was planning my work as a union shop steward: how to handle a pigheaded boss or a willful worker—a far cry from anything creative. The freerunning horse in the field gets a different kind of exercise from the circus horse going round and round the ring, *one* two three, *one* two three.

The cold autumn of 1933 had one good effect. The Spies, which were inclined to color poorly in streaks and splotches, fairly blazed under the touch of the frost. Spies are late in producing, late in blooming, and late in maturing their fruit. When we began picking them in mid-October, their leaves were still as green as in summer. The weather grew steadily colder, the sun weaker, and often there was a skim of ice on Freya's water dish in the morning. One evening as the shadows lengthened among the trees, we shivered even in our heavy clothes, and back at the barn we could see our breath.

When I came back from town the thermometer stood at twenty-seven, and when I went to bed, twenty-three, with the stars blazing winter-bright in a windless sky. I slept poorly, worrying about the Spies still on the trees, the windfalls on the ground. In the morning it was fifteen, the ground hard as iron and Freya's water frozen clear to the bottom. Before I went to town I went out into the orchard. At first glance all was as it had been, the leaves green and the apples bright among them. I picked a fallen apple from the ground. It looked glazed with a too bright, unhealthy sheen: hard as a rock, frozen solid. Disgusted, I threw it down.

I reached in among the green leaves to pick a fruit, and the leaves clattered like bits of metal, frozen stiff on the branch. I had never seen anything like it. The fruit on the low branches was glazed, but not as badly as that on the ground, and the apples from ten feet up to the top of the tree seemed to be fine. I did not know what to do. But there was a barnful of Spies from yesterday. The doors had been closed and they were all right, so I went to get the men.

On the way I stopped at Goodale Orchard and caught the manager in the middle of breakfast. I described what I had seen.

"Do you suppose they are ruined?" I asked in conclusion.

"The windfalls are for sure," he said. "Did you have many?"

"Quite a few, Greenings and Spies and some Russets."

"Well, they're gone. No good even for cider. They'll soften right up when the sun gets to them."

"What about the Spies still on the trees? We've only got in about half of them."

"Those, I would think, are probably all right. It used to get this cold down in Maine when I was there. The farmers didn't touch the fruit while it was frosted on the tree, just let the frost work out naturally, and unless it stayed cold for several days in a row they came out all right. It's going to warm up some." He looked out the window, and we could see a haze over the faraway hills beyond the marsh. "I should think they'd be all right."

"I surely hope so," I said.

"This has been a tough year, and the worst is yet to come. The last time it was this cold this early was the winter of '18. Lot of peach trees killed that year. Still, you can't tell. It might warm right up and stay pleasant till Christmas."

It did warm during the day, enough to film the ground with a thin, slippery layer of mud and to thaw the apples slowly. When the sun touched the trees the frozen leaves withered and lost their color; a breath of wind brought them down in showers. By evening the apples hung like Christmas tree ornaments from the bare branches. The glass that night did not fall below thirty, and the apples were safe. They will stand a temperature of twenty-nine or a little below, on account of their sugar content. We hurried to get them off before the crazy weather could produce another catastrophe.

The last few days Joe and I worked alone. Stanley and Kassie had heard of a possible job that might last through the winter—something to do with the government, they said. We had neither the time nor the right mood for a farewell party this year, and were all depressed as we stood in the barn door on their last evening. The incessant north wind roared through the bare trees, and the old timbers creaked like a ship struggling in a seaway.

"It's been really tough this year," I said, "and I can't thank you boys enough for standing by me the way you have. We are a good team, and I hope we will all be together next year."

"Oh, next year . . . ," said Kassie, and shrugged. "Who knows?"

"They say the welfare is almost out of money," Stanley added. "Louis's wife has been on all summer, had to with the old man sick. Last time they didn't want to give her anything, but when she cried they did give her a three-dollar food coupon, and said she would have to make it last for a week. Four in the family and nobody working."

"What did she do?"

"Kassie gave her his last week's pay," Stanley said. "We went short at the house but we got by. They're way behind on the rent. But the bank didn't take the house yet. Got too many now, I guess."

"This new president down in Washington, this Roosevelt, is a friend of the poor people, they say," Joe observed. "I read in the paper where he's going to find work for us, and if he can't find it he's going to make it."

"I read that, too," I said. "Perhaps this job that Stanley and Kassie heard about is the beginning of something like that. The money is going to be distributed to the towns to be spent on improvements that they couldn't afford otherwise—roads, sidewalks, things like that."

"Sounds all right," Stanley said. "It could be something like you say. All I know, they have an office over in Salem, my cousin told me, some kind of letters on the door. CWA or something like that."

"That's it, CWA, Civil Works Administration. They don't waste much time. They only got the money last May. Get right after it. It might be something really good."

"Let me know what you hear, will you," Joe said. "We're up against it down my house, too."

The next day Joe and I worked across the road where there were four small Baldwin trees that for some reason were out of tune with the others and had a heavy crop. Baldwins would be fine if it were not for their in-again, out-again habits, but no amount of feeding, mulching, or pruning could make them change their ways. I had fed the Baldwins a double dose of expensive nitrate of soda the year before, hoping to encourage the growth of fruit buds, but they just gobbled it up and converted it into rich, dark leaves and stout new wood.

It was a miserable day, sunless and raw, with heavy clouds driving from the north and a biting wind. We walked back to the house at noon, a forlorn procession, Joe and I hunched and shivering, and Freya slouching along behind with her tail between her legs. We had been having dinner in the kitchen all fall; the barn was much too cold.

"I don't know what you'll do when the wintertime comes, poor doggie," Joe said to Freya. "Or what the rest of us will do, either."

I shoved the kettle over the burner of the stove. "*Soupe aux pois,* again," I said. "The whole kettleful only cost a dime, so you don't need to worry about taking some. Get a couple of bowls out of the cupboard, will you?"

"I've got my dinner here," he protested.

"I know you have, but you need more than one sandwich and a cup of tea to keep warm out there this afternoon. I guess that's why we're cold all the time. We don't eat enough."

"Could be," he agreed. "I notice I'm warm right after I eat, but it wears off after a while."

"I thought things were better at your house," I said. "From what you said yesterday, they don't sound so. What's wrong?"

"Oh, just about everything," he said, and tried to grin. "The state job folded up in July, and my cousin Maurice, who lives with us, has had nothing to do since. My mother worked for the hotel a whole month for nothing. When she tried to get her money they said they didn't have it and there was no more job anyway."

"What about the Wildcats?"

"We haven't been doing so good, either. Business was rotten at the beaches. We did have some work at the Dance Hall, but when the boss tried to cut us down, Kip got sore. He'd had a few anyway, and he punched the feller in the nose, and they wrassled all over the dance floor. We got him out of there before they called the cops, but we didn't get our money for that night, and no more work there, either. The last time we played was Saturday before Labor Day in Newburyport. I guess Kip had it all figured out, because we never did see him after the show. He just took off with the dough. Had some friend waiting for him outside, probably. Most likely he went to New York: he was always talking about it and growling about 'the hick towns.' So—no more Wildcats. Fortier and Bernie got disgusted. Bernie hocked his horn and they went to Quebec, back to the woods. I don't know if we would have had anything this winter anyway, things are so bad."

"It sounds like you had an awful summer. Why didn't you tell me?"

"What more could you have done? You've done plenty for us already. Anyway, the summer was not bad: Maurice and the kids got us fish and clams and vegetables from somewhere.

Probably they swiped them; I don't know and I didn't ask. Times like these, it's awful hard to stay honest."

"You do."

"So far, yes. But I don't know if I could always, if I saw my mother and the kids hungry. I thought last fall, when my mother had to go to the welfare, why don't I just go out and stick up somebody, a gas station or something. You know why I didn't? No nerve, that's why."

"Is that why?"

"Well, mostly," he said, and laughed.

"Some more soup?"

"No, thanks. It was awful good, though. I've been talking plenty about me. What about you? How are you going to make out, do you think?"

"All right, I think—I hope—if nothing happens. We're a thousand boxes short of last year, on account of the Baldwins mostly, but everything is good: no small ones, no green ones. If we can average two dollars across the board I shall be all right with something to start next year. I won't get ahead, but I won't fall behind either. Just hold my own. I wish I could get a stake together so that a bad break wouldn't ruin me. Just think what would have happened if we hadn't got those Macs before the storm."

"It doesn't look like you're going to get rich any more than me," Joe observed. "If you were being paid by the hour it wouldn't come to much, would it? Well, we're in the same boat, got to row or sink."

"Then I suppose we had better get rowing," I said, looking at my watch.

The next morning as we were finishing I said to Joe, "Do you know anything about digging wells?"

"Some," he replied. "Sullivan Brothers that I used to work for did it sometimes, and I worked on one or two. Most times they drill for them. Drive a pipe with a point on it. Cheaper that way."

"But they used to dig them," I persisted. "The old ones I've seen, about four feet across and stoned-up inside, they must have been dug."

"Oh, they were, sure. But why?"

"Well," I said slowly, "I was thinking last night. If we could dig a well and find some decent water, even if only enough for a summer supply for the house, it would put an end to a lot of trouble. I'm seven hundred dollars behind on what I expected in rent this year. Most of the trouble is the water, I'm sure. If word gets around that the water supply is no good then someday the house won't rent at all, and I'll be sunk with taxes and insurance to pay."

"Where would you try?"

"All the good water seems to be on the south sides of the hills, and there is supposed to be a running spring in the marsh somewhere near the island. I would try in that fold of the southeast field and try to hit the vein leading to the spring. The only thing is, could we do it in the winter?"

"You could, by beginning right away quick before the ground freezes deep. You could thaw the surface by building a fire on it and keep it soft by stacking mulch over the hole at night. But you'd best have it drilled; then you wouldn't have to pay if they didn't find water."

"I'd rather pay a little more and make work for us—that is, if you think the two of us could do it? With three thousand bushels of apples in the cellar I should be able to gamble three hundred dollars on such a project. Of course if we found water it would cost a lot more, for pipe and a pump and pumphouse. We shouldn't have to pay for rocks. There are plenty of those in the old stone walls. So, do you think we could do it?"

Joe dropped his bag of apples on the ground and walked over to where I stood. His face was dark with anger, his eyes blazing.

"You're only doing this for charity," he said, violently. "Well, I don't want any charity work, not from you, I don't."

"Don't be so silly," I said, angry in my turn. "I don't want any damn drillers around here. My father had plenty of them and they stuck him, too. They never even tried down here where I want to, and he could have dug ten wells for the price of that saltwater one. If you don't want to do it, just say so, but let's have no more fool talk about charity."

"That's all you're doing it for, I know," he insisted.

"Listen, don't be a damn fool. I told you what the idea was. If you aren't interested, let's forget it. I don't want to fight with you, not about this, not about anything. But there is one more thing, though. I shan't have hardly a thing to do this winter, and I will go nuts sitting in the kitchen till spring. Did you think of that? Cool off and think it over and let me know what you decide."

I turned away, moved my ladder, and went back up to get the last bag of apples. From the next tree, there was silence. We loaded the trailer and I drove up to the barn, Joe perched on the tailboard and Freya following.

He was waiting when I shut the motor off. "I'm sorry I was so ugly," he said, his eyes filled with tears. "I don't know what is the matter with me, I get sore like that. If you want to dig a well, we'll do it, sure."

"Swell," I said. "Now you know about this, and I don't. What will we need?"

He wiped his eyes on the worn sleeve of his jacket. "A damn fool, you're right," he said. "All we want to start is two shovels—a long-handled and a short-handled—and a pick. You have those. And some boards to cover the hole, and some mulch. Later you'll have to have a suction pump. Probably you can borrow one. When do you want to start?"

"Why not tomorrow?" I asked. "We've got a couple more hours with these Baldwins, and I would like to cover the hedge in front of the house, and then we'll be all set."

The hedge was a treasure: small-leaved box, growing far to the north of its native place. It grew along the front of the house, curving gracefully in toward the white front door with its carved pilasters. Sitting on the granite block that was the front step in the warm spring sunshine, I used to sniff the spicy fragrance of the shiny leaves. It was as much a part of the house as the old red lilac and the giant linden: all three were foreigners, after all.

It was four feet high and almost as thick. The stout little trunks were feathered to the ground like the feet of the bantam chickens I had owned as a child. Last year I had not covered the hedge, and it had come unscathed through the warm winter. But this year was something else again, and I dared not take a chance. From under the barn we got out the old doors used for the purpose and discovered a cache of boards that would be just the thing for shoring up and covering the well.

We drove stakes around the hedge to hold the doors, tipping them until they met over the hedge in a V.

"It's pretty," Joe said, running a hand gently over the bright leaves. "Does it have flowers?"

"No, just leaves. It grows so slowly. Would you think it is just as old as I am? Thirty-two years. I feel sort of related to it somehow. It was planted the year and month I was born."

"The French people say," Joe remarked, "that if a tree is planted when a child is born, they grow along together. If one gets sick so does the other, and they even die together sometimes."

"Quite a responsibility for both of them," I said.

The next day we began the well, and I could see that Joe knew what he was doing. I had not chosen the place entirely at random, for an engineer friend of some bygone tenants had said that he thought it was a likely spot, and I had remembered. Fortunately it was on the south slope, sheltered from the wind that still blew relentlessly from the north. The frost struck down only a few inches, and on the edge of the marsh there was a convenient pile of dry peach brush, which we dragged up and fired over the spot that Joe had marked out.

While it was burning we brought up two big loads of mulch and a load of boards and two-by-fours from an abandoned henhouse. Before dinner the ground had softened and the coals cooled enough so that Joe could begin digging. He began at the outside of a five-foot circle, cutting through the soft sod as though it were cheese and tossing the clods well back from the hole. I sat and watched and fooled with Freya. After a while, I said, "You stop now and have a smoke and let me try."

"There'll be plenty for you later. Sit down while you can."

"No, I want to try. I'm getting cold and it looks so easy."

He handed me the shovel with a grin and sat down on the mulch pile to watch. I stabbed at the tough sod and had to jump on the shoulders of the shovel and work it back and forth to make it cut. I thought I had loosened a good clod, but only a little divot broke off with all my effort. I tossed it away in disgust and tried again.

"How do you do it?" I panted at last. Joe's cigarette was smoked down to the butt, while I had chewed out only a ragged little hole. "Show me."

"I just shovel, that's all, like this," he said, and once more he began cutting smoothly and evenly through the sod. Each stroke bit to the full depth of the shovel; each clod was detached cleanly and left a shiny little cliff of loam. Try as I might, I could never do it. My job would be to keep the earth well back from the edges of the hole, and this was plenty to keep me warm, as it turned out.

At first there was nothing to it. I puttered around with a rake; lots of time to stand and look around. Above us was the peach orchard, the orderly rows thick with stout red branches; between the rows, the asparagus with feathery foliage, brown now, which I should have to cut down sometime before spring. Below us was the oak island, the trees still flying their little mahogany flags. The squirrels, in an acorn-hoarding frenzy, were chattering and jerking their tails. Beyond the island stretched the marsh, dun-colored and flat as a floor to the faraway hills and the dunes of the sea beach. Occasionally a stab of sunshine broke through the clouds, but mostly it was a gray day, chilly and sad.

By noon Joe had shoveled out three feet of loam and was well into stony yellow hardpan, but he went through this almost as fast and with tireless rhythm.

"We shouldn't have to go deeper than eighteen or twenty feet," I said, as we walked up to the house at noon. "At the rate you're going it shouldn't be long."

"You can't count on going this fast," he warned. "When we get down five, six feet we'll have to shore her up to keep her from caving. Then, by and by, we'll build a platform, and I'll toss dirt up on it for you to shovel out. And then we'll have to haul it up in a bucket. The deeper we go, the slower, and if we strike ledge—" He shrugged his shoulders.

"There's no ledge, I'm sure of that," I said. "Boulders, maybe, and clay."

"Boulders we can handle with the tractor and block and fall. Clay is bad. How deep do you think, five feet, six?"

"I don't know. Maybe."

He shook his head. "That will go slow. You have to go under the clay to find the water. It comes only in gravel or sand." In mid-afternoon he struck clay, and I saw what he meant. The slippery gray stuff was packed so hard he had to loosen it with the pick. It clung to the shovels and the edges of the hole and clotted on our feet. We quit at four; it was growing dark and we had to cover the hole. The wind had dropped. It would be a cold night.

"Climb down here," Joe said. "I want to show you something." Five feet down in the solid clay were earthworm burrows, each with its soft, pink occupant curled at the bottom.

"Never seen them so deep. Must be a very cold winter coming up for sure. Five feet of frost."

"Ah," I scoffed. "How could they tell?"

"They know," Joe said. "Five feet of frost, you'll see."

Day by day he inched deeper, and the raw clay pile built up around the hole. I slipped and struggled to keep it shoveled back. The grass, the tools, and our clothes were slimed with the stuff. Freya, disgusted, moved away and burrowed herself a nest in the mulch pile. I was thrilled when I saw dribbles and trickles seeping out from the clay walls.

"Look, water," I shouted. "I knew we'd find it."

"Nothing but seepage," Joe grunted. "Tomorrow we knock off digging and shore her up. And you'll have to begin pumping."

Tomorrow was none too soon. That afternoon, with a loud sucking sound, a portion of the wall let go. Joe scrambled to get clear, but before he could reach the ladder the slide caught him, burying him to midthigh.

"Take it easy now," he directed, as I scrambled with my shovel to get him free. "You move too fast, you'll start her sliding again and bury us both." I was panic-stricken, seven feet down in the hole with the cracks opening all around us, but I tried to move gingerly and to avoid touching the wall. It seemed ages before he could work his legs free and we raced up the ladder.

He laughed shakily. "Scared, are you?"

"I'll say," I gasped.

"Me, too," he said. "I saw two of Sullivan's men buried in a cave-in. They were smothered before we could get them out."

"I wish we'd never started this," I said. "I never thought it would be so dangerous. Probably there's no water here anyway."

"There may be," Joe said reassuringly. "And it will be safe enough when we build a wall of boards to hold back the clay."

Next morning when we removed the covering of mulch and boards we found the hole two feet deep with thick, gray water. There had also been further slides of clay during the night. Before we could shovel or shore we had to set up the suction pump that I had borrowed from the highway department and pump for fifteen minutes.

The pump consisted of a heavy iron basin with a lip, a diaphragm worked by a log handle, and several lengths of two-inch hose, with more to add as the hole grew deeper. The leverage of the handle made it easy to operate, and it developed a tremendous suction. Water, clay, and even pebbles poured over the lip and ran away in a turgid stream through the grass.

Once the hole was dry, Joe cleaned it out, and we spent several days bracing the sides with the stoutest timbers and boards that we could find. He built a platform at the six-foot level on which I could stand. Because of the cave-in, the hole had increased in diameter to more than eight feet, and there was plenty of room for us both to work.

Every day we picked and shoveled. Joe tossed the clay onto the platform, I struggled it over the top, and we took turns scraping it away from the edge. Each shovelful of clay was handled three times at least. The raw stuff, veined with frost and piled into mountain peaks like the beginning of the world, sheltered us from the wind, but it also kept the low sun out of the hole. In spite of the chilly dampness we worked in shirt-sleeves and slapped our jackets over clay-slimed clothes only when we came to the surface.

Our hopes soared when, at the twelve-foot level, we struck gravel, but it was a dry vein. I was on the surface when I heard Joe curse.

"Look here now, look at this," he said, disgustedly.

He was foreshortened to pygmy size at the bottom of the hole. His face was gray, his black hair stood in clayey peaks and tufts, his dungarees looked stiff enough to stand alone. He had shoveled the gravel onto the platform, and as I looked down he made an angry stab with the pick.

"Never have I seen anything like this, never, by Gar. Blue clay, and hard—look!" He swung the pick with all his strength, the muscles knotting on his short arms and broad back.

Thunk, it went, *thunk, thunk, thunk,* and each stroke dislodged only a lump the size of a tennis ball.

"Eight feet of clay already and now this. If there is much of it we will be here till spring."

Joe was rarely discouraged, but now he scrambled out of the hole and plunked down on the mulch pile, irritably scraping the clay from his boots with a stick.

I was wishing with all my heart that we had never started. Well, he had tried to warn me, and I had been too obstinate to listen. But on the other hand, I thought to myself, the little wad of bills that I had handed him each week had meant food for his family. What would he have done otherwise? There had been no word from Kassie and Stanley. For my own part, I had been interested by every step in the project. Only the weekends were required for the apple business: shipment, correspondence, and bookkeeping. The rest of the time I should have sat in the kitchen or sawed wood alone, always alone. It was not even the first of December yet; so many long months till spring.

I looked at my watch. "It's quarter of," I said. "What say we go up to the house and eat and decide what to do."

"NOW," I SAID, after we had eaten, "what do you think?"

"It's not up to me to think, that's your job. You know what you can afford better than I do." He grinned to take the sting out of the words and waited quietly, smoking and stirring his coffee while I thought.

"I can't afford to quit," I said at last. "We've spent so much time and money already that there is nothing else to do but keep going and hope for the best. If we hit water it will be all worthwhile. Otherwise we might as well have taken a hundred-dollar bill out into the field and buried it."

"I think so, too," he agreed. "Now, this is what we should do. This afternoon we'll take out the platform and build a thing like this." He sketched a tripod on the oilcloth with his thumbnail. "Then we'll both pick, you as much as you can, till we get as much loose as possible. Then I'll shovel it into the bucket and you haul it up on the pulley and dump it. It will go quicker so."

That was how we did it. Daily we worked down deeper and deeper. The weather favored us. It stayed cold, but clear—no rain, no snow. By mid-December the mark on the stick showed seventeen feet.

"If we don't hit it at twenty feet we might as well call it a day," I said, as we covered the hole.

The next morning Joe added an extra length to the suction hose of the pump and set it more firmly on its platform of boards.

"This is the day," he said excitedly. "You stay up there by the pump. Just you watch."

He began picking—*thunk, thunk.* The point penetrated two or three inches at each stroke and dislodged the usual little ball of clay.

Suddenly he gave an exultant cry. "By Gar, there she is." The pick blade was buried to the handle, and as he withdrew it, the water bubbled up through the hole. "Pump," he shouted, "pump fast, and empty the bucket as quick as you can!"

The clearing water bubbled over the lip of the pump mixed with grains of coarse black sand. I dipped in a finger and tasted it. It was sweet.

We had to get the plumbers then, and tile. Joe had said he didn't know how to do the rock work and thought this way would be best and cheapest in the end. We took turns pumping while we waited and at last saw the truck, with four men aboard, jouncing toward us over the frozen ground. On the platform the lengths of red tile pipe, four feet across, were wedged and roped. It was three o'clock when they began laying the bottom tile, while Joe pumped to keep the hole dry so they could work, and nine o'clock at night when the last one was in place. We worked by the truck headlights, using our block and fall and the power take-off of the tractor. As I came down over the field with coffee and sandwiches, I could see the immense bulk of the boss plumber and hear his bellowing voice. It was a windless night of cold and brilliant stars.

The next morning Joe was back to wind up the job. The shoring lumber was thrown any which way like jackstraws; picks, shovels, and crowbars covered with clay were scattered around. We had brought glasses from the house, and before we began on the mess we dipped up a bucket of cloudy water and solemnly drank to each other, to good luck and good health. It was an achievement, it really was. Even the boss plumber admitted that.

We piled boards over the well, stacked it deep with mulch, anchored that with more boards, loaded the remaining lumber and the tools on the trailer, and headed for the barn. As we came over the crest of the hill, the wind cut our faces like a knife. Our eyes and noses streamed. In the kitchen the beans cooled on our plates before we could eat them, and the thermometer in the north window stood at ten degrees.

"You're going to be awful cold in here this winter," Joe observed. "Remember the earthworms. I shan't like thinking of you here all alone."

"Oh, I'll be all right," I said easily. "I got along fine last year. I'll bank the house with mulch. That will make a big difference."

"Maybe," he said doubtfully.

"What about you?" I asked.

"Well, I can tell you now. I didn't want to before, afraid you'd make me quit before we finished the well. The government job has started. Maurice is working already cutting brush up River Road. They've got a big gang there. Going to build a new strip of road to take out that bad curve near the bridge. They need a guy to drive the truck, and that's me. I start tomorrow."

"Good, swell," I said. "But you shouldn't have taken a chance on a thing like that. We could have waited on the well."

"That's what I thought you'd say, so I didn't tell you. Anyway, it's all right. Three days a week at five dollars a day. And snow shoveling for the town between times. If it keeps up maybe I can marry my girl and have a place of my own. She's getting tired of waiting. Broke off with me last summer, but we're back together again now. Better times are coming, I know it."

I could not see it myself. It looked like a long while until spring.

At the town square we shook hands, "Goodbye, my friend," Joe said. "Be seeing you. Take care." And he walked away.

IN THE MORNING the thermometer stood at zero. Frost lay thick on the windowpanes and on the nap of my blanket. There seemed little to get up for. I wished I could lie curled in my nest until spring, like a woodchuck or a bear. Finally I put my feet down on the freezing floor and scuttled down the hall to the bathroom. There, at least, it was warm. A portable kerosene stove had been stinking away all night; happily, the water ran when I turned on the faucet, and I heard the rainwater pump start up in the laundry downstairs.

Usually in our latitude the autumn days are chilly and damp, with southerly and easterly winds off the ocean bringing in fog or downpours of rain, but no real cold until after Christmas. This year we were square in the middle of a wind tunnel to the Arctic, and day after day the gales roared out of cloudless skies and the frost struck deeper and deeper into the snowless ground.

It was several days before I could turn the crank on the tractor, which I had unwisely left in the open shed next to the apple cellar. No sun reached there to soften the grease and oil. I wanted to collect some mulch (the kitchen was freezing), but it was not till I drained off the oil into buckets and heated it all morning on the kitchen stove that I could finally get the machine started. I found the mulch frozen, even along the south slope, and I had to pry up great stiff rafts of the stuff and pile it like cordwood in the trailer. Even though I stamped it down along the north wall of the kitchen, it had lost much of its insulation value. It needed days of thaw to soften it for packing down, but there were none.

As Christmas approached I began to wonder what to do about the family. Where could I make a place warm enough for us to sit? The dining room had French doors, and no cellar under it; even with a roaring fire on the hearth, in such weather it would be impossible. My brother must have sensed how things would be, for a week before Christmas he called up on the telephone and said we all had been invited to some cousins' for the day; and what about it? With relief, I replied that it would be fine. I would see them there on Christmas Day.

But again the weather took a hand. Two days before Christmas it was so dark in the morning that I thought my alarm clock must have gone off too soon. (I still set the alarm clock, even though there was nothing to get up for; I felt I should get demoralized if I lay abed.) I lit a match and looked at the clock. Seven, and still dark as the grave.

It was much warmer, and there was no sound of wind in the larch branches. In the kitchen, Freya was still curled up on the sofa. She opened a sleepy eye as I lit the room, then with a sigh burrowed deeper into the cushion. It was the first time she had been warm in a long time, and she was determined to make the most of it. I pulled the kettle of oatmeal forward on the stove, got out a pan of baked apples and a can of milk, and carefully measured the precious coffee into the pot. I opened my book, propped it up on the ink bottle, and sat down to eat.

There was a little gray light to outline the small window-panes, but it was still very dark. Suddenly, a gust of wind shook the house, sighed through the linden branches, and died away. I carried my dishes to the sink and went out into the yard. It was still as death, so quiet I could hear the scrape and rumble of ice cakes in the tide and, far away, the mournful whistle of a train engine: two long, two short, blowing for a crossing. There was a light, cold touch on my cheek, on my forehead . . . snow.

I backed the truck out of the shed and drove it down to the kitchen door where I left it while I went in to take inventory of the food closet. Plenty of salt, sugar, coffee, and milk, but if I were to be snowed in for days I should need tea, oatmeal, pota-toes, peas for soup, and prunes. I was so sick of apples I could hardly look at them; prunes would be a change, and cheap. I still had carrots and cabbages in the cellar. I wished I had got the parsnips dug before frost, but I had forgotten. They would overwinter and taste good in the spring. I drooled at the thought of them, and dandelion greens, and asparagus. Too much of my thinking was concerned with food, I decided, but I went right on dreaming of clam chowder, impossible now that the flats were frozen, and steak and melons and squab. In my mind's eye I could see my father carrying up the bed tray when I was a sick child, unfolding the legs, and setting it down. There, on a piece of buttery toast, was the delicious lit-tle brown bird, all for me.

"Stop it, cut it out," I said aloud. Freya looked up guiltily to see what she had done.

Still, if I were going to shovel snow, I should need meat; part of a pork loin would be cheap and good. And Freya's meal bag was almost empty. I looked in my wallet. There were a few dollars there, enough. I was really busted. I had paid the bank another thousand dollars—foolishly perhaps, but it made me feel safer—and the balance of taxes and insurance, and Joe for the well. But I expected several checks on the first of January, including a good big one from Mr. Moss.

There were still two thousand boxes of apples in the cellar. Thanksgiving business had been good, Christmas too, and though prices had not improved over the year before, Mr. Greenberg was hopeful that they would pick up after the new year. There had been no trouble keeping the cellar cold; it had stayed at twenty-nine for over a month now.

The heavy snow still held off as I came back from town. There were fine flakes like mist in the air. Distant outlines were blurred, and thin white snakes of drift hurried across the road, whipped by a rising wind. Even in the barn I could hear the rumble of the sea like a train speeding down a faraway track. There was a sense of hurry and excitement. I stowed away the food in jig time, brought in several loads of wood from the barn in the wheelbarrow, stacked it in the wood closet, and braced the northeast door of the barn with a timber. As I came back to the house I noticed that the wheelbarrow track was almost obliterated. I built a big fire in the dining room fireplace. There I should sit and watch the storm through the wide French doors. Let her roar: I was ready, even to the shovel and snowshoes on the back porch.

Roar she did, and howled and moaned. The snow drove against the windowpanes of the east door like sand and sifted down into the garden on the lee side, piling up inch by inch, hour by hour, against the glass. One by one the landmarks vanished: first the bare oaks of the island, then the spruces of the windbreak. At last the barn itself was only a shadow in the swirl of flakes. The fireplace gobbled up wood in the rush of draft; the wind boomed in the chimney; the house creaked and trembled in the blast. I loved it. I went all day from window to window, marveling at the mounting waves of drift. By midafternoon the road was filled solid between the stone walls. There was not a light, not a track, as darkness fell.

By the middle of the next morning it had blown clear. Now the northwest wind took over and hurried the snow into fresh waves of drift. The bright air was shimmering with flying flakes. New spots were blown bare, and a monster drift covered the driveway and streamed across the road. The telephone operator said that the road was packed solid for four miles, too deep to plough. A gang was digging but making slow progress. The loose snow filled in almost as fast as they could shovel. My Christmas would be right here, I could see, and spent shoveling. It would take two days or three to open the road, longer if the wind continued.

I didn't care. I wasn't even disappointed about Christmas. I have always liked to shovel snow, and I began systematically at the road end of the driveway where there was least wind, cutting out the wind-packed blocks and tossing them clear behind me. As I got chilled I went in to the house and ate soup or coffee. My excavation was neat and shoulder-deep by noon, but it went nowhere. It ended in a cliff that was the road.

In the afternoon I put on the snowshoes and walked a mile or two toward town with Freya rocking along behind. Our tracks were the only ones on all the sea of snow, and even from the hill-top I could see no sign of shovelers. The drifts were tremendous. Only the telephone poles marked the course of the road. The wind was dropping, and it was coming in bitter cold. As I followed my webbed tracks back toward home I began to feel desolate, as if I were the only person living in the world.

While I was eating supper that Christmas Eve Freya jumped up and woofed and bristled. Then her tail began to wag, and the next minute I heard feet stamping on the porch. The door opened, and in came Joe.

"Joyeux Noël," he said. "I saw your light."

"Boy, I'm glad to see you. Have some supper? How did you get here? You look a *vrai coureur des bois,* I must say. Come on, have a pork chop, don't argue. This is like old times, and mighty nice. Now sit down and tell me all about everything."

He took off his brightly striped stocking cap and his sash and his mackinaw, on which the snow was beginning to melt, and hung them back of the stove.

I sliced off another chop and dropped it in the pan.

"I'm on the shoveling gang," he said. "I told them I wanted to work on this road, and that was all right. No one else did—windiest place in town up there. I thought we might get down here by dark, but they're still more than a mile away. So when no one was looking I stuck my shovel in the drift and just took off across the fields. I'd brought my snowshoes just in case. I saw your tracks and Freya's, so I knew you must be here."

"Where else would I be?"

"I thought you might have gone somewhere for Christmas. I would have come anyway to see to Freya and that things were all right. Oh yes, and my mother sent you a present." He fished a damp package out of his mackinaw pocket. She had made me a pair of red mittens with bright green Christmas trees on the backs.

"She wanted you to have Christmas dinner with us, too," he said, "but they won't have the road open, I don't think. The guys don't want to work on Christmas Day, and the drifts are ten feet deep along by the pond."

"I'll come on snowshoes," I said. "That would be fun."

"I could meet you after church," he said. "We're going to have a turkey, she said to tell you."

"I wouldn't care if it was baked beans," I said.

"My kid sister Del won it in a raffle, what do you know," he said. "When they gave it to her, she bust right out crying and ran all the way home with it, no paper on it or nothing. When they saw her all the kids started bawling; you'd of thought someone had died. Oh yes, I almost forgot: I brought you something else." Again he fished in the mackinaw pocket and brought out a package.

"This is from me," he said, shyly. "I wish it was more."

It was a pint of whisky.

"Gee, thanks," I said, delighted. "We'll have some right now. It will taste great after all that shoveling."

"Not much of a present, and I drink it up," he grinned as I poured him a glass.

"Not all for you," I said, filling mine.

We emptied the bottle before he had to go back to work.

I went out into the shed while he put on his snowshoes.

"It's a wonderful thing to have a friend like you," I said in French. "Whatever happens, I'll never forget how kind you've been."

"That works both ways," he said in English. *"Joyeux Noël.* See you tomorrow somewhere on the road."

"No matter what turns up, this has been worth it," I thought muzzily to myself before I fell asleep. "Such nice people, the LaPlantes, the Greenbergs, Mr. Moss, everybody. . . ." And, bang! It was morning.

Christmas morning, and not a breath of wind, even at dawn. Close to zero it was, the snow pink in the low sun swinging up from the southeast. Not a sign of open water in all the wide marsh; not a track on the snow-blocked road, except ours of yesterday. Not a sound. Even the sea was quiet on the sandbar. Rosy clouds of frost smoke hung over the open water.

Indoors I made a great bustle and clatter, slamming about with breakfast, fooling with Freya till she barked and scrabbled with her claws on the linoleum. This was a different Christmas from any other, so there were no thoughts of the past. I filled the stove, looked to the harness on my snowshoes, and went to the telephone.

First I called up the family to wish them Merry Christmas. My mother sounded so concerned that my high spirits were dampened.

"Oh, no," I said, "everything is fine here. Sure, plenty warm. I'm having dinner with friends up town. No, the road isn't open. I'm going on snowshoes. Apples? They're all right: a couple thousand boxes. Yeah, keeping fine. Well, Merry Christmas, and love to the cousins. Have fun. Oh, sure, I'll have a good time: I'm looking forward to it."

I felt a shamed relief to have that over with. Today I didn't want to think of the past, the future, apples, money, anything but the bright moment—the sun, the snow, and the gay friendly people. No complications, no worries . . . just for today.

I shut the door in Freya's wistful face and swung away easily over the drifts. I had told Joe I would take the old road to town and save a mile, so I set out along the ridge by the windbreak, crossed a strip of marsh and a salt creek, hard frozen now, and mounted the easy slope of the first low hill. As I passed the pond I could hear the ice rumbling and groaning as it froze ever deeper under its white blanket. A squirrel jumped in the branches of a pine and shook down a puff of soft snow. There was a lacework of mouse tracks near a wild apple in a pasture. A seagull sailed in slow circles over the marsh and glittered in the sun. From the causeway I could see the distant spires and roofs of town and, far away, a solitary black speck. Joe was coming to meet me.

We met where the causeway joined the upland and swung along side by side, following the half-obliterated track of the abandoned road. As we talked and laughed, our breath trailed behind us in the clear air.

"I am glad you could come, Bateese, my friend," he had said when we met. Joe and Baptiste were characters in a French Pat-and-Mike saga, and I had laughed over their adventures, amorous and ridiculous. Since he was Joe, I must necessarily be "Bateese," and so I had been for a long time.

We stopped at the drugstore where I picked up a box of candy for the children and two bottles of real French sauterne that the liquor dealer had left there for me when he came downtown to get his newspaper. On his own, he had Christmas-wrapped them.

The LaPlantes lived in half of a mud-colored wooden house in the part of town called Frenchville. An ugly house, but not today in the snow and the sun. As we leaned our snowshoes against the front porch rail, Mrs. LaPlante opened the door.

"*Joyeux Noël,* Merry Christmas," she greeted us.

Mrs. LaPlante's brown face was as wrinkled as a Russet apple in April, but every line and wrinkle was a kindly one: not a worry mark or a frown line anywhere. Her small, bright black eyes laughed up at me. I towered over her—over all the family—and took up more than my share of the space in the crowded room. She smiled with pleasure when she saw her mittens.

"The best and warmest I've ever had," I said.

"It's because my sister sent me the wool from Canada, from Quebec," she explained. "The poor sheep there must grow the good wool, or else they freeze, poor things. Joe, find your friend a chair and introduce the children. I must watch Del's turkey or he'll burn."

There were three chairs, a stool, some boxes, a little table covered with a cloth, and a sagging cot that did double duty as a sofa. I was shown to the place of honor, the armchair between the stove and the Christmas tree, and sat there feeling rather silly while the children were brought up, one by one. There were six of them: three LaPlantes: Adele, nine; Jenny, eleven; and Xavier, thirteen; and the three orphan Belangers: Paul, ten; and the twins, Francis and Rose, who were eleven.

The LaPlantes were all black-eyed and black-haired, but the Belangers were fair, Rose a real blond with golden hair and blue eyes. The little girls all curtsied, and the boys bowed when they were introduced. Rose and Jenny went out to the kitchen to help, and the others sat in a demure row on the cot. Joe perched on a box, while cousin Maurice and Xavier took the chairs. The wood fire crackled in the stove, and the white winter sunlight poured in through the curtainless windows and fell upon the holy picture of the Virgin on the wall, the crucifix on a shelf in the corner, and the Christmas tree with its strings of cranberries and popcorn.

"Your turkey smells wonderful, Del," Xavier remarked, sniffing. "I'm so hungry I could eat him up all by myself."

"No, you could not. He's awful big, even if he did only cost a dime. You know," she said to me, "I had just one ticket with the dime a lady gave me for watching her baby outside the store. Most everybody else bought three for a quarter. One man got a whole book; I saw him. And then Father Bernard called out, 'Number 611, Adele LaPlante, has won the turkey!'"

"And she just stood there like a dope," Xavier laughed. "I had to give her a push, or they'd have given it to someone else."

"She came home bawling," Paul observed.

"You did some bawling yourself, big shot," Maurice reminded him.

"The tree looks awfully pretty," I said.

"Maurice and I cut it in the woods," Xavier said, proudly. "And the cranberries we found last fall. The girls popped the corn in the stove, and we all made the strings. It should have lights, though, don't you think? But we don't have electricity."

"I think it looks fine just the way it is," I said.

"Dinner's ready," Jenny announced, and we all trooped into the kitchen.

It took three tablecloths to cover the plank table. There were boxes to sit on; the china did not match. There were jelly tumblers for the cider and wine, but all the same, it was most festive. The monster brown turkey was at one end. There were cranberry jelly and bowls of gravy and dishes of onions, carrots, turnips, and potatoes. The children just stood and stared in awed silence, and then in a rush everyone sat down and we all fell to eating and drinking and laughing and talking. The children followed up the pie with candy, while the grown-ups opened the second bottle of wine. The children finished the dishes and went out. We sat there until the steam had cleared from the window and the low sun told me I must be on my way.

"Thank you for the nicest Christmas ever," I said to Mrs. LaPlante. "Whatever happens, I'll not forget today."

"Whatever happens will be good, you'll see," she said. "Someday I'll tell your fortune, only you mustn't tell Father Bernard. I am so often right he thinks it's the devil's work. But for you, I see good times coming. Some trouble yet, then good times."

"She does hit it right a lot of times," Joe observed as we walked along. "She knew when the tree fell on my father in the woods, and when Father Bernard came to tell her, she told him,

'You do not have to say anything. I saw the great tree fall, and I know that my husband is dead.' Do you believe that?"

"Sure, if you say so. But really, an accident in the woods several hundred miles away? How could she see it?"

"I don't know," Joe said. "But it happened like I tell you. And other things, too. She is wrong about one thing, though. She says I will marry a tall blond girl and move away from here. My girl is dark, and we will live here if we marry. I don't even know any tall blond girl, so how could it be?"

"I don't think I believe in any of it really," I said. "It must be chance or coincidence."

We walked along in silence for a while, the only sound the squeak of our snowshoes on the snow. It was very cold but windless. The last of the afterglow had faded, but the bright winter stars gave light enough to show our tracks of the morning. We came to the place where we had met and I stopped, took off my mittens, and fished out my pack of cigarettes.

"Let's sit down on the wall and have a quick smoke," I said. "This is as far as you go."

He protested, but I overruled him. "You'll get enough exercise tomorrow on the road. I can find my way, don't worry. You could put me down here blindfolded and I could get home. The stars give plenty of light."

"Aren't you afraid, way out there all alone? I would be."

"Afraid of what? A *loup-garou?* A ghost?"

"Maybe."

I laughed. "I'm sure any ghost that I might see would be a friendly one. When I went down at night to turn on the pump, I used to hope to meet my father under the trees, but I never did. Yes, if there were ghosts, I should have seen one then."

"Wouldn't you have been scared if you had?"

"No, I don't think so. I think I'd have liked it."

A tree cracked loudly in the frost, and we both jumped and laughed.

"Let's change the subject," I said, "or you'll have to walk back with me after all, and I don't want you to. I do hope your mother realizes how much I enjoyed Christmas and how much I appreciate her asking me."

"She knows," Joe said. "At first she was worried about no furniture and like that, but not after she saw you. I told her this was one millionaire that wouldn't mind sitting on a box."

"This 'millionaire' is getting cold," I said. "I had a wonderful day. See you tomorrow, perhaps, if it doesn't snow again."

"Sure. Not a *loup-garou* this side of Quebec."

I did think of ghosts and werewolves a few times on the way home, but forgot them when I opened the back door and Freya came bounding to meet me. She cried over me and scrabbled and stood up with her paws on my shoulders and kissed my face with her warm tongue. I dished her up a big bowl of meal and water, ate a saucer of prunes myself, and we both went contentedly to bed in the quiet house.

In New England, February is the most dismal month of the year—short dark days and a weak sun without power. A few dispiriting days of fog settled on the snow, and I hoped for an open winter after all. Then the wind whipped around to the north and blew a bitter gale straight from the pole. All day the glass dropped steadily: ten to five to zero and, at sundown, to five below and still descending. At sunset the wind slacked off, but with the coming of darkness it picked up again. It roared in the chimney and tore at the elms and the linden. The ground beneath them was littered with twigs and small branches.

All day I had sat lethargically huddled on the sofa, moving only to get myself some soup or a slice of bread. Although the sofa was close to the stove and I was dressed in a heavy flannel shirt, wool pants, and two pairs of wool socks, I was chilly. The colder I grew, the less my inclination to move. I did not go to bed, just dozed, curled close to Freya as the windy hours passed.

I must have slept, because when I started up half-frozen, my watch showed two-thirty in the morning. The kitchen was so cold that I thought the stove must have gone out, though it had not. I went into the laundry and turned the faucet in the tub. No water came. I scraped the frost from the window and turned the flashlight on the thermometer: the thin red line had retreated so far down toward the bulb that I could hardly see it, and when I did I could not believe it: nineteen below and still blowing. It would fall even lower when the wind dropped and the cold air settled down.

The soup in the kettle on the back of the stove was barely warm. I pulled it forward and went over to the sink to get a drink of water. None there, and the few drops that had collected around the drain were frozen solid. Probably all the weak old pipes would burst, I thought. Well, I would shut off everything, dig out the cistern cover in the morning, and dip the water out in a bucket. At the prospect of doing something, I felt better. The soup was hot, and I ladled out a bowlful. As I ate, my mind worked again.

Nineteen below. I had seen it colder in the mountains, but it was dry there. You didn't feel it so much. Boston Harbor must be frozen over, I thought, and Gloucester. What had the Burnhams done when it got like this? Sat in the fireplace, probably.

There was plenty of wood then. And the Bay Colony people, and the Plymouth settlers? How did they ever stand it? How they must have longed for England. Suddenly a thought occurred to me that made me lay down my spoon: the apples in the cellar!

I left the rest of the soup congealing in the bowl and began putting on my parka and heavy boots. Outside, the wind took my breath away. Head down and stopping to turn my back, I made my way toward the barn. I did not dare open the north door of the cellar, so I pried up the trap door and prepared to slide down the chute, flashlight in hand. The cellar felt warm and smelt sickeningly of apples. Probably everything was all right. The walls and ceiling were heavily insulated, surely enough to keep the temperature above the crucial twenty-nine-degree mark.

I lit the lights and made my way down the aisle of boxes to the east wall where the thermometer hung. I almost fainted when I read it, then turned the flashlight on it to make sure. It read twenty-six. And that at the point farthest from the door.

There were a few open boxes of Spies along the west wall. I picked out several apples at random. They looked unhealthy, glazed. They were frozen. In storage they would not recover as they had on the trees. I did not kid myself, they were gone. But the packed boxes might be saved if I could raise the temperature before the cold could penetrate the insulating paper.

There were eighteen hundred boxes left, more than thirty-five hundred dollars. I scrambled up the chute, dashed back to the house, through the cold dining room and hall and up the attic stairs. In a frenzy I began dragging blankets out of the chests, scattering the mothballs in every direction. The heavy

Hudson Bay blankets that my father had brought from Canada, the big double ones, the white ones with black stripes, and the thick red ones—I dragged them roughly over the splintery floor. It took three trips to get them all out to the barn.

Last of all I brought the ones from my bed and the little portable kerosene stove from the useless bathroom. I set it up in the middle of the floor and lit it, but I had no faith that the tiny thing would do any good in that vast space. The cold must be coming in somewhere—everywhere, probably. The blankets covered perhaps three hundred boxes of the best three-inch Macs, the big red ones we had picked in the north orchard the day of the storm. I made two more trips to the house and dragged out the rugs from the living room and the library.

Then, exhausted but warm, I sat down on a box and looked at my watch. It was quarter past four. At five-thirty I roused myself and consulted the thermometer. It had gone no lower; perhaps it had even gone up a shade, I could not be sure. I sat down on the floor and, leaning against the chute with my head on my knees, I fell asleep. When I awoke it was quarter past seven. The cellar thermometer stood at twenty-seven. The stinking little stove had done some good, after all. Perhaps if the weather moderated something could be salvaged. But when I came out into the daylight, the cold seemed to freeze my lungs when I drew breath. The wind had dropped, and the thermometer in the kitchen window stood at minus twenty-four.

Although the sun shone brightly all day the temperature did not rise more than three or four degrees, and toward night it began going down again. I spent a miserable, restless day, half-dozing on the sofa under one old quilt I had kept out for myself. Twice I went out to the barn cellar, filled the stove, and checked the thermometer, noting hopelessly that it was down to twenty-five, and then at nightfall to twenty-three. I had tried to start the truck in the vague hope of getting another stove somewhere, but the engine would not turn over. Not a soul went by the house all day. The telephone did not ring; I found out later that it was out of order. Joe was sick in bed, but he had sent Xavier down to the corner with a nickel to call me up. There was no answer.

For my part I had no wish to talk to anyone. What could I say? My head ached and I felt sick. It took me a while to get up enough of my own steam to dig out the cistern and dip up a bucket of icy water. I saw my haggard reflection without interest before I dropped the iron cover back with a clang.

Afterward I stood at the kitchen window for a long time, cooling my hot forehead against the glass. What if, I remember thinking, this is the return of the ice age and the glaciers come sliding down from the north, burying first the fragile peach trees, then the apples, and finally, the house itself, till only the tall chimneys show above the ice. Hungry and always cold, you think strange things. Perhaps, like Admiral Byrd alone in his hut in Antarctica, I was poisoned by the fumes of the oil stove, but I think it more likely that he and I both were victims of loneliness and despair. I slept on the kitchen sofa under the ragged quilt, chilly and cramped and troubled by nightmares.

Eventually the weather moderated, and I came back to life when the thermometer climbed to thirty-two. It seemed a useless gesture to open the cellar to warm it up, but I did so. In the light of a gray morning I pulled a box of Macs out from under the blankets and dragged it over to the door. I pried up the slats with the pinch bar, unwrapped an apple from the top layer, and bit into it. The flesh was juicy and crisp, cold but not frozen. There were three hundred twenty boxes under the blankets and rugs. To be on the safe side I should have to repack them all. If I could salvage those I could pay everything and have about one hundred dollars left. No more money till August or September brought the peaches. I should be worse off than when I started, because although I had no old bills, I had no stake either. The last of the yawl money had been spent on that defiant gesture to the bank.

I never felt hopeless unless I was hungry or cold or had nothing to do. Now I was no hungrier than usual, I was not cold, and I had the apples to repack. With the door open to let in the cloudy daylight I began on them, and as I slipped into the rhythm I tried to plan for the future. I should get hold of Mr. Greenberg to see if he could sell the frozen apples before they rotted.

Fifteen hundred bushels would make a lot of cider. Who would drink all that? At ten cents a bushel, one hundred fifty dollars, or was it fifteen dollars? No, the extra zero on the ten made it one hundred fifty. It didn't make much difference anyway. At two dollars, it would have been three thousand. Why had this happened to me? Had I been too cocksure, arrogant? Well, if that was it, if I was being punished for something, there must be a cross God somewhere watching me, like the one I used to imagine as a child, who always saw me when my hand was in the cookie jar. There were plenty of people who believed there was such a God—Joe for one, probably. I had never asked him.

Well, I could not imagine a God who had nothing better to do than to punish a poor little character on a pocket handkerchief of land. It was possible to be reasonable and yet not have a reason for the way things happened. The whole weather pattern of the Northeast had not been changed just to punish me and a few other sinners. The thing to figure out was not why it had happened but what to do.

At noon I went into the house to eat and telephoned Mr. Greenberg. The kitchen was warm, and in the middle of the linoleum was a lake. A pipe had burst. Well, I thought, it's lucky I shut off the pump or all the water in the cistern would have been pouring down from the ceiling. This was just draining from the line. I had mopped it up, eaten dinner, and was waiting for Mr. Greenberg to arrive when the telephone rang. I was not pleased to hear my brother's voice.

"Well," he said. "Where on earth have you been? I've been trying to get you all yesterday and last evening."

"Oh, I've been right here. The telephone was out. They just fixed it this morning."

"How cold was it down there?"

"Twenty-four below. Even colder up town and inland."

"Good lord. How did you make out? Did anything freeze?"

"A pipe in the kitchen burst a while ago. It is the only one I know of so far, but some of them are still frozen, so I can't be sure."

"How about the apples?"

There was no use lying about it, so I said, "The apples, oh, they froze."

"What?"

"I said, 'They froze.' "

There was a silence. Then he said, "All of them?"

"Not all, no. About three hundred boxes are all right."

"How many did you lose?"

"About fifteen hundred."

"Fifteen hundred bushels, good God! What are you going to do now?"

"I don't know. I'll think of something."

There was such a long silence that I thought we were cut off when he said, "I think we had better come down on Saturday and talk this thing over. We just can't go on like this. Even if we could borrow enough money to keep the farm going, there would be no sense in it. We'll have to make some decision."

"I might be able to get a job to see it through until the peaches," I said hopefully.

"A job. There aren't any jobs. You know that. And as for the peaches, don't you even read the papers, for heaven's sake?"

"Not lately, no. Why, what about the peaches?"

"The peach crop is gone as far south as New Jersey. The buds have all been killed, and most of the trees, too. You'd better look at yours."

"I will, this afternoon. Perhaps they are all right. So near the sea, you know."

"I doubt it. Well, we'll see you Saturday on the early train."

Under the sullen gray sky I plodded through the snow down to the peach orchard. The brushy little trees looked sturdy and vigorous, their scarlet twigs bright in the dismal landscape. I could not believe there was anything wrong with them. From strategic spots along the marsh, along the wall, and from the middle rows I picked blossom buds and placed them in an envelope. For good measure I clipped some small branches to force in the house.

I spread the buds out on paper on the kitchen table and, with a sharp knife, carefully bisected one. Inside the brown sheath it was a fresh bright green, and I rejoiced. But, wait—there at the very center was a brown spot, hardly larger than a fly speck: the embryo blossom, and it was dead. The cold had penetrated the sheath, the leaf layers, and had killed the sensitive heart. I opened another and another. All were the same, all dead. Savagely I crumpled the paper and crammed it, buds and all, into the wastebasket.

I had been dry-eyed at my father's funeral and through all the events before and after it, but now I threw myself down on the sofa and, with my arms around Freya, I wept without shame. She sat unmoving, her face wrinkled with concern, while I sobbed and wailed, not for the loss of all I had worked for, not for the apples frozen in their boxes, but at the thought of April without peach blossoms! Finally, I stopped and watched the last tear thread through the tawny hairs of Freya's coat and drip down onto the sofa cushion. She turned her head then and licked my cheek with her warm tongue.

"What a business, hey, Freya?" I said hoarsely. "Well, don't worry, I'm okay now, or I will be when I have some coffee."

She thumped her tail on the cushion, then sighed and curled up in the corner, keeping a watchful eye on me as I pulled the kettle over the fire and got out the coffeepot and cups. Mr. Greenberg drove up to the door just as the kettle boiled.

"You timed that well," I said to him. "I was just going to have coffee, and your cup is all ready for you."

Once in the kitchen, he put a gentle hand on my shoulder.

"What is it? What has happened?" he asked.

The friendly concern in his homely face brought the lump back into my throat, but I swallowed it down and said, with an attempt to laugh, "Oh, just about everything awful that you can think of. I'll tell you all about it when I make this coffee. Sit down there by the window."

He listened quietly while I told him the whole story. From time to time, he shook his head, and after I had finished he stirred his coffee and took a swallow before he spoke.

"I can unload the frozen apples if they aren't too bad. The vinegar factory up in Middleton will take them all, I think. But if I get you a dime for them, it will be lucky."

"I didn't figure they'd be worth over that," I said. "They've thawed out. They aren't rotten, just very soft and mealy."

"They'll go quick, though. The mill will take anything that isn't more than half-rotten, but I should move them right away. We should clean them all up this week in case it snows again."

"That would wreck us for sure," I agreed. "There must be an end to this run of bad luck sometime, but maybe not yet."

"At a dime it would be only one hundred and fifty dollars. What are you going to do?"

"My brother asked me that. I just can't imagine. I wish I hadn't given that thousand to the bank; it would have seen me through. On the other hand, the bank might have foreclosed if I hadn't paid. They could have anyway. I just don't know."

"The banks aren't so interested in foreclosing. Still, this is a good property. They might have. Good house lots. Did you ever think of that?"

"My brother has, you can bet, and the bank man mentioned it, too. But I'm not interested. I just want to keep it as near what it has always been as possible."

"Nothing stays 'what it has always been' anymore," he observed. "You are foolish to try, I think."

"You're right, of course," I said. "I have been gradually coming to see that it can't last forever as a farm, even with luck. But I don't want to let it go. It is the only thing that keeps us together as a family, and even though nobody else thinks so now, I'm sure that someday one of us will be able to swing it. I wanted to hold it until that day came, and this seemed to be the only way."

"That I can understand," he said. "The feeling for family is strong in the Jewish people. Not so strong in America, I think, and that is bad. Without the family, there is nothing. But if your family feels as you do, they should be helping you now. It is too much for you alone."

"That's just it, they don't see it my way right now," I explained. "To them it's just a hopeless situation. I had a hard time persuading them to let me even try it when my father died. They were all in favor of letting the bank take it right then. Besides, they can't help me. It's all they can do to help themselves, that and pay their share of the debt. I took on the bills that were outstanding here, but there were plenty of others. My father was sick a long time before he died, but he kept on struggling and never believed that he could not come back. That's what happened, plus the fact that people never paid what they owed him and he never hounded them for it. This Depression can't last forever, and I just want to hang on to this place until better times. Do you think I'm just being stupid and stubborn about it?"

" 'Stubborn,' yes. 'Stupid,' no," he said. "How much would it take to get you through next year's harvest? A thousand dollars?"

"If the house rented, and if I let the bills run, and if I did almost all the work myself—so many ifs—yes, I could do it."

"I could let you have a thousand," he said suddenly. "Not for business, for friendship."

I sat in stunned silence. The lightning thought went through my head: this is the finest thing that has ever happened in all my life. What I have learned this minute I shall never forget. People are essentially good and kind—I might have spent a lifetime and never found it out. I felt a surge of exultation, as though I could spring up and jump over the sofa and chairs. If I had been a little more French and a little less New England, I should have sung and shouted. But I only sat quietly and said, "Thanks, Mr. Greenberg, but no, I can't do it. If the place belonged to me instead of to my mother, you would have some security, but as it is, I couldn't let you take the risk. You are very generous. I'll never forget it, never, as long as I live."

"If you change your mind, let me know," he said. "Let me know what happens anyway. And now we should look at the apples."

It was a gloomy meeting at the early train. My brothers looked very citified as they came down the passenger car steps. They also looked stern. Long afterward, they told me how much they had dreaded this interview, but I did not know of the hours of discussion that had preceded it. To me they looked severe and cold, and they saw only determination and hostility in my face. They commented on the height of the snow banks piled alongside the road, and I made desultory replies. It was a gloomy, sunless day. There was no color in the landscape to raise our spirits, which were not improved by passing Mr. Greenberg's loaded truck heading toward town.

"There go the last of them," I observed. "In one night they dropped in value from two dollars to a dime. Must be some sort of a record. Even in '29 you couldn't lose money that fast."

"Remember the Mississippi flood when Mother was a young girl in Louisiana," my older brother reminded me. "When you think of it, is it any wonder that she feels as she does about agriculture? It is unthinkable that she should go through another catastrophe like that. She is worrying herself sick over it, and it has got to stop; that's all there's to it."

I made no reply. They had me, and we all knew it. Selfishly, I had not thought of this angle, and yet it was the only one against which I had no defense. It had been fifty years since the Mississippi had burst through the levee and the yellow floodwaters had spread devastation and ruin over the fertile acres of Belmont plantation. The exciting story that we had never tired of hearing when we were children was being relived in a New England variation, stripped of its glamour.

It had a quite different significance in this setting than when I used to lie snug and safe in my warm bed and follow it in all its detail to the end. The tawny river, swollen with the rains of half a continent, ran high, higher than the roof of the plantation house, crowding with irresistible force against the levee that alone held it back from the cane fields and the rice fields with their elaborate network of irrigation ditches.

From the gallery the family had watched the men working in the red glare of torches and heard shouts above the roar of the river as the men struggled frantically to bolster with sandbags the weak points of the dike, the crawfish and rat holes where the probing fingers of water poked through. First a few drops seeped through the grass, then a trickle. At last, with a rush and a roar, the levee began to crumble all along the big bend above the plantation, like our sand forts on the beach when the tide came in.

The men ran for their lives then, and the yellow water crawled across the fields toward the house. The family stayed. When the water crept under the front door and poured across the rosewood floor of the dining room, they went upstairs. When it found them there, they climbed out on the roof. There they sat huddled like terrified sailors on the disabled hulk of a ship. At last a rescue party in a boat took them away across the flooded acres to higher ground. When the water receded, the restless river had cut a new channel. The house and most of the land were drowned. In the ruined fields, the fast-growing willows took over. My mother always finished the story, "And for years afterward the passengers on the steamboats could see the columns of the house standing in the middle of the river."

As we drove along in silence I thought that it had been a river that destroyed my hopes, too—a river of Arctic air pouring down from the North Pole without even the frail barrier of a levee to stem the flow. No wonder my mother sickened as she saw history repeat itself.

We sat around the kitchen table and drank coffee. I had dipped water out of the cistern that morning and had filled the boiler on the back of the stove. Two brimming buckets stood in the corner of the laundry. I should get along without plumbing until spring. Plenty of people had done so in this house before me.

My younger brother did most of the talking.

"Farming is a risky business at best," he said. "And you have undertaken the impossible, without capital and in a place where both taxes and labor costs are so high that you can't compete. In our store we sell Southern apples in baskets for a dollar. Pretty good they are, too. Can you do that?"

"No," I said. "And I don't see how farmers in the South can do it, either. They have freight charges that we do not. They must lose money on every basket."

"Of course they don't, or they wouldn't stay in business. For one thing, they pay their help seventy-five cents a day. Their taxes are negligible, and for all I know they don't have the blights and insects we do. This has never been a real farming area, and it never will be. There is no sense in beating your head against the wall."

"People have farmed here for over two hundred years," I offered.

"And where are they now?" he said impatiently. "They scratched out a bare existence when the soil was virgin, and they were smart enough to sell out when the going got too tough. This place is going to be residential land for commuters or rich estates. You can't change the inevitable just because you want it otherwise. There is no sense in arguing."

"Don't worry, I am not going to argue," I said, and I saw them glance at each other in surprise. They looked positively relieved when I continued, "What do you think we had better do?"

"I see no way but to sell," my younger brother said. "I have a possible customer for four acres, residential. I am asking a thousand dollars an acre."

"That much!" I exclaimed.

"In good times we could get it easily. Even now, it looks promising. If we could do it, we should not have to be in a hurry to sell the house and the rest of the land. We could hold it for a really good price."

I swallowed and asked, "What piece of land do you mean?"

"The peach orchard."

"Oh, no," I burst out. "Why, that has the new well on it and the asparagus bed."

"The well is what might do it. The asparagus doesn't matter one way or the other. Probably they wouldn't want to bother with it. How about the peach trees, are they all dead?"

"None of them are. Just the buds were killed."

"Well, I don't know whether it would matter whether they were or not. They might be an asset, I don't know."

I said nothing. Remembering my grandmother's advice, "Keep your tongue between your teeth," I bit back a rush of words. Unsentimental and businesslike, they talked on and on about house lots and boundaries and planned an illustrated brochure describing the Colonial features of the house. I looked out the window and wished that they would leave. Without protest, I agreed that I should stay on to wind everything up. This time the spring would be an end, not a beginning.

My brother was right; there was no argument. If I had been alone, with only myself to consider, I should have stayed with the farm to the end. But as things were, it was hopeless and I knew it. We sat silent. I do not know what they were thinking. I thought of Mr. Greenberg. He had been uprooted when he was too young to protest and had been tossed around so that he had never had a chance to firm up. He was fluid enough to roll away from the fingers of fate like a drop of mercury on a dish.

It was ironic that he should regret that same quality in his children. Was it a kindness to let children solidify so that a blow to the world they had known would smash them? He deplored the restlessness that accompanied the uncertainty of their life, yet perhaps it was for the best. It would be fun to talk about it.

At the thought of Mr. Greenberg, of his homely face with its kind and troubled eye, it occurred to me as quick as a dream: This is your harvest, the beginnings of sympathy and understanding of people. But it is only the beginning, Lesson One in the book, and all the other chapters are to follow. And in spite of myself, I felt a stirring of curiosity and eagerness to turn the page and see what lay in Chapter Two. In that instant, my grip began to relax.

Capricious nature can also be kind. I have little memory of the weeks that followed. I know that it was cold—continuously, everlastingly cold—and that I felt dull and hopeless. I'll bet there are few people who understood Admiral Byrd's book *Alone* any better than I did, how there is a disintegration of the mind that comes with being constantly cold and with no one to talk to. It was a great effort to go to bed at night and an even greater one to get up in the morning. I did it, though, and ate and washed once in a while and dragged water out of the cistern and filled the stove and fed Freya. But what I felt and thought about, if anything, I cannot remember. It is helpful when enduring pain to know that there will be no memory of it afterward.

Even a potato in a bag in the grocery store knows that it is spring. I knew it, too, when I stood in the backyard the first warm day in March and stretched in the sun and yawned and looked around me, awake at last after a long sleep. The snow was really melting. A patch of mud had appeared in the garden between the shrunken drifts. Once I knew a Newfoundland girl who told me that in her town the children, winter sick, used to go out on the first warm days and dig down through the snow to the earth, just to reassure themselves that it was really there.

Freya and I sunned ourselves on the south side of the house all that morning. There was hardly wind enough to stir the trailing branches of the elm. The marshes were still iced over, but they had lost their steely glitter. The ice was rotten, and the first high tide and strong wind would sweep it away. Already a tongue of blue water showed in the river channel above the bend. If this was really the beginning of spring, Joe would be coming out of the woods. He had gone down to Maine with a logging crew just after Christmas, and except for his paycheck (which arrived every week from the company office), his mother had heard nothing from him. He would be sorry to learn what had happened to the farm. But he could pick up road work when the frost was out of the ground. By that time I, too, should have a job. This was my last idle day.

Freya watched with troubled eyes my preparations to go out job-hunting, and she followed me everywhere through the house, her nails clicking on the bare floors and the worn treads of the attic stairs. My trunk was in the corner where I had shoved it when I first came home. I had never unpacked it or looked into it, beyond tossing in some mothballs to discourage the squirrels. Fortunately they had left it alone. The white pellets had all but disappeared, though their smell remained to mingle with the warm, musty smell of the wide pine boards of the roof.

For two years I had worn only dungarees and sneakers or wool pants and boots. I should feel silly in a skirt and silk stockings. I wished that I had unpacked before. Everything was creased and crumpled. I had tossed my things together hastily, with a heavy heart, I remembered, when I left my good job in the Hartford Museum to come home. There was no sense in thinking of another museum job. The Depression had hit them hard, and anyone who had a university job was hanging on to it like grim Death. I did not feel up to seeing Mr. Moss and telling him my hard-luck story. Newspapers and magazines were out of the question, too. Their staffs had been cut to the bone. Even in the good times when I had first started to work, the publishing houses had been impossible to crack: I remembered a sharp-eyed personnel woman, with glasses on a black string, who had said to me, "In this business you have to wait for someone to die, and no one here is even sick!"

The choice, then, narrowed down to the mills and factories, quite a few of which were still struggling along in the county. Optimistically, I felt that the only requirements for these jobs would be strength and willingness to work; besides, I should be thrown in with the type of people whose language I had been speaking for the last two years—that is, when I was speaking at all. At this thought I felt less shy and cheerfully dug into the contents of the trunk.

For a person with a good job, I had had a very limited wardrobe, I discovered. My extravagances had run to theater and concert tickets, ski trips to the mountains, and vacation tours of Europe. There was, however, a brown gabardine suit only slightly shiny, a really good pair of shoes, a few blouses that were not too bad, some stockings—most of which appeared to have runs in them—and a brown corduroy suit, which turned out to have a large smear of India ink down the front. There was also a green velvet evening dress and gold slippers, which I carried downstairs for laughs. I did not think my new life would include this ensemble, but it might amuse Freya. She was embarrassed when she saw me in it, and so was I when I looked in the mirror.

Knots of muscle stood out on my arms and shoulders, and last year's tan line was still quite unattractively visible. I tossed the finery to one side and turned to the suit. I should be sunk if I could no longer get into it. Certainly it did not fit as it used to, even last year at the Greenbergs'. The skirt was loose and the jacket tight, but it looked all right, or would when I pressed it and got myself cleaned up.

As there was still no plumbing, this was quite an undertaking. I had found an old-fashioned, round tin tub in the attic. It was too big to fit on the stove, so I heated the water in buckets and filled it. The windows steamed over so that I was hidden from the prying eyes of the birds. Freya was in an agony of modesty and mortification as I soaped and splashed in the middle of the kitchen floor, and she scrabbled away when I pretended to pull her in with me. I looked quite fine, I thought, when I was finished. There was still some afternoon left. No time like the present. Locking the drooping Freya in the kitchen, I went out and climbed into the truck.

I began in Newburyport, to the north, and visited three shoe factories that afternoon. I had planned to put off trying the only industry left in my town, a stocking mill, until the very end, and only then if all other places were hopeless. I could not bear the thought of sympathetic or curious looks and questions. My own approach was impersonal, and that was what I wanted in return. And that was what I got, in Newburyport and everywhere else.

At the first place I joined four other women on a bench in a dirty, dark room with chipped matchboard walls. Three were elderly, with seamed round faces and scanty hair strained back from their foreheads. They glanced at me as I came in, then went on talking Polish in sad, complaining voices. The fourth was young, thin, with powder caked over bad skin and hands like claws with bitten nails. She moved over to make room for me, and I grinned at her. After a moment she smiled back, and we began talking.

"You gonna sign up here?" she asked.

"Yeah, I thought I would. How are chances?"

"Well, I been signed over a year now and had about five weeks work out of it is all I know. Still, you can't tell. They hire when they feel like it and who they please. Heard they took on some last week, so I thought I'd come around and let them know I'm still alive."

"What do they pay?"

"Thirty-seven."

"Dollars a week?"

"Cents an hour."

"Oh," I said, embarrassed.

"You can get a week's pay out of it, when you work," she explained.

"No union?"

"Nope. They let you know if the union comes in they'll fold altogether. The organizers used to come around and hold meetings and like that, but nobody joined. Didn't dare to. Now they don't come anymore. Better not mention union where any of these jerks can hear you, or you'll go to hell before you ever get hired."

The personnel clerk who had been typing with her back to us yanked the paper out of her machine. The three Polish women stopped talking and looked toward her hopefully. She turned around and appeared to see us for the first time.

"No work today," she said indifferently. "Next week, maybe, or the week after."

One old woman translated to the others, and with resignation they began to button their coats. My companion on the bench nudged me.

"Tell her you want a card," she whispered.

Without looking at me the clerk fished a card out of the drawer and pushed it and a pencil toward me. There was not much to fill out. Name, address, telephone, and pay expected. I put down thirty-seven cents.

I hesitated over the last line: name of last employer and pay received. Then I naïvely wrote down "Hartford Museum, $50 a week." I did that in quite a few places before I got wise and put down the name of the orchard and fifty cents an hour. It didn't make any difference anyway. I didn't get one inquiry from any of them.

The clerk took my card and, without looking at it, tossed it into a wire basket with some others.

"Nothing today," she said to my companion. Without another word she turned a page in her shorthand book and began to type from her notes.

As we walked down the dirty staircase I said, "Did anyone ever get a job from one of those cards, do you think?"

"No one I ever heard of. The only way is to be there when they're hiring and up near the head of the line. It's different for stitchers. That's skilled work, and they make good dough. But there's too many of them, so you got to be a real brownnose to get a job stitching. Well, there's always the Gimme Store, though they ain't had anything but prunes there lately. Be seein' ya."

On the way to the next place, I went by the "Gimme Store" on Elm Street: SURPLUS COMMODITIES was written over the door. A long line of women with bags and baskets stretched away from it down the block. You never knew what was going to be government surplus that day: sometimes it was prunes, sometimes flour or potatoes. It was food, anyway, and free. I didn't get anything there myself, but I knew lots of people who did, and they said it was good stuff.

During the next days and weeks I went to every factory within commuting distance of the farm. Not one was hiring, although outside the employment offices of some there were long lines waiting in the sun or rain. Always it turned out to have been just a rumor of work that had brought us all there, and after we had stood for an hour or two someone came out and told us to go away. At last, rounding the full circle, I came back to my own town, and the one interview I dreaded.

Our local mill was a modern building, clean, bright, and airy, but inside the same conditions of long hours and low wages prevailed. In addition the proprietor, whom I knew by reputation as a hard man, did his own hiring, and there was no way of avoiding an interview with him. I was more nervous in his bright office than in all the other dingy places put together, and I waited and fidgeted on the shiny bench. At last he appeared, a big man with shrewd eyes cold as stones in his fat, red face. He looked me over with disapproving recognition and waited to see what I wanted.

New England seacoast towns were steeped in the snobbish hierarchy of the sea, developing a social order with merchants and ships' captains at the top and common sailors and artisans at the bottom. When shipping vanished and industry grew up, the old system continued with mill owners at the top and immigrant mill workers at the bottom. The mill owners' social position was unchallenged until "city people" began to move in and buy up abandoned farms. They were usually seasonal visitors, unaware of and uninterested in the town's social structure, and their indifference was seen as a challenge and an insult. This resentment began at the top and spread through all ranks of the town. Although I joked with Joe about the millionaires on Argilla Road, I had never taken these hard feelings seriously. I had plenty of troubles, but concern for my social position was not one of them. To the mill owner, however, I was a fine example of how the mighty were fallen, and he made the most of it.

He opened the conversation by saying smoothly, "What can I do for you, young lady?"

"Young lady" was a neat, deliberate touch and reduced me to the status of a dilettante jobhunter looking for a few weeks' work to see how the other half lives.

Only once have I felt a similar anger and embarrassment, and that was when, years later, I looked up from my place on the Sylvania assembly line to see a woman I went to school with being taken on tour by the plant manager. She spied me at once, and as she started moving toward me the line boss called out "Change over" and the belt stopped moving for a few minutes.

I was well and truly caught, with no excuse not to talk to her. The other women on the line drank in every detail of her appearance and every word she said. She began by some reminiscences of boarding school and then continued, "How *interesting* to find you here, but then you always did do unusual things, didn't you? I suppose you are going to write a book about labor problems or something." Purple with embarrassment, stammering something, I almost died when she added, looking coolly around her, "Why, some of these girls are really quite attractive, aren't they?" Fortunately none of my friends held this against me, although they did tease me about my pal, "Mrs. Richbitch."

To the mill owner I blurted out, "I want a job."

His reaction was as unexpected as it was infuriating. He burst out laughing.

I stood it as long as I could, and then I said, "What's so funny?"

He did not answer this but asked instead, "What do you want a job for?"

"Why does anyone want a job? So I can eat."

"Yes, yes, of course. I did hear something . . . too bad, too bad. Well, I hardly think a job here would do for you."

"Why not?" I asked sharply.

"Well, for one thing, the help here start at half past six in the morning. A little early for you that would be, wouldn't it?"

"I am used to starting at half past four," I said shortly.

"This would be different. And there are other reasons, of course. . . ."

"What reasons?"

"I just don't think it would do at all. You would not be satisfied, for one thing, and I like to have the help satisfied. We are a happy family here—no labor troubles, no union, nothing like that."

Aha, I thought, so that's it. He thinks I must be a labor organizer. A guilty conscience, I'll bet. And the idea occurred to me, probably that was what everyone in all the mills had thought, if they thought of me at all. It was something to consider. If there was such a fear on one side, there must be the need on the other. I knew little about unions and distrusted what I did know, but if the shoe fit, I might put it on sometime.

"So you have nothing for me?" I asked.

"I'm afraid not, no."

"Okay," I said. "Goodbye." And I left.

But once I was outside in the truck, the memory of his laughter burned away everything else. The fool, the oaf. More than a job, more than anything at that moment, I needed a beer and a friend to share it. And there on the sidewalk stood Joe.

"Hi, Bateese!" he shouted, and waved his arm.

I brought the truck to a stop with a squeal of brakes.

"Well, the old lumberjack himself. Where's your beard? I thought you'd be tripping over it by this time."

"I had a good one, I tell you. But when I'd been in the city a week, Portland, I found a beard didn't go so good there. The barber pretty near had to use a lawnmower to get it off. The kids at the house were all sore. They'll hardly speak to me, they are so disappointed."

"What say we go get a pitcher of beer?" I suggested. "Where's the nearest place?"

"The Riverside, I guess. Kind of a tough joint but the beer is good. Ever been there?"

"Never have, no. Don't know where it is, even."

"I'll show you," he said, getting in. "Down that way."

The brown water of the river, still running high, washed close by the tumbledown frame building. The bar was to the right as you went in. Everything was very quiet. A couple of old barflies mumbled together on their stools.

"We'll take a private room where we can talk," Joe said, leading me past the bar and up a short, dark flight of stairs. He opened the door marked "Number 11" in tarnished letters. Inside were a table and chairs; a dirty window overlooked the river and the fields beyond.

"Seems like a whorehouse," I observed.

"It used to be, in good times," he said. "I hear you had a rough winter. They say the place is for sale, is that right?"

"That's right," I said, and told him all about it.

He listened quietly. When I came to the night when the apples froze, he gasped under his breath, and looked down. I continued to the end while he drew circles and triangles in the spilled beer with a stubby forefinger. When I finished neither of us said anything for a while.

Then unexpectedly he asked, "What about the hedge that we covered up with the doors last fall. Did it come through all right?"

"It's funny you should mention that: I was just thinking about it. I waited till last week to uncover it, and when I took the doors off it was lovely and green. But when I ran my hand over it I thought it felt dry, and the leaves rustled in a funny way. After a couple of days in the sun it began to turn brown, and now every leaf is off. There is nothing left but sticks. It's stone dead."

"What, all of it?" he exclaimed, shocked.

"Not quite all, as a matter of fact. A big drift of snow covered about three feet of it at the southwest corner of the house. Some branches were broken when the snow settled, but it is all right and beginning to grow."

He heaved a sigh of relief.

Then I remembered, and I had to laugh. "That means I am saved, I guess. This time, anyway. Born to be hanged, probably."

He looked seriously at me, then said stubbornly, "Just the same, it is good some part of it came through alive."

Then he went to the door and hollered down the stairs, "Hey, Tony, another pitcher."

As we idled through the second pitcher he told me about his winter in the woods. As he talked I could hear the whine of the saws and the ring of the axes, the voices of the men sharp in the intense, dry cold of the forest. The great pines swayed on the stump before they began to fall. Then in a flurry of warning shouts they toppled and, gathering speed, came crashing down. Before the tree had ceased to quiver the toppers were swarming over it, gay in mackinaws, sashes, and knitted toques, laughing and swearing as they stripped off the feathery limbs.

EPILOGUE

What happened next in my mother's life? Here the manuscript breaks off, and no one now alive knows. I imagine she finished her beer and, warmed by her conversation with Joe, drove home alone to Freya. The days would have gone on more or less the same—pruning, spraying, picking—and become years. Her heart must have sunk by cruel, slow degrees as each day confirmed the inescapable reality: the little orchard could not survive in such hard times.

Increasingly convinced that farming would not work, her brothers quietly made efforts behind the scenes to sell the farm for their mother's support. In 1936 the entire property—the orchard, the main house and barn, and the summer cottage—was finally put up for sale, with a fancy brochure and a price of ten thousand dollars. That would have covered the 1931 and earlier mortgages with a little left over. There were no offers.

So, the orchard staggered along as the Depression kept its tight grip on Ipswich. By 1935, the WPA had begun providing white-collar jobs, and during the farm's off-seasons Kitty obtained employment as part of a team writing an area history. It was a very anxious period; she went from day to day, she told me, not wanting or even daring to think ahead.

Her life changed greatly when one day in 1936, on the way to town after a day of spraying, she gave a ride to a stranger walking along the road. Years later his mother told me she thought her son had brought home a male friend: it could not be a woman, she said, dressed in dirty work clothes, deep-tanned, and with such a short haircut. That September they were married and moved to a neighboring town. The following June I was born: their only child.

My parents could hardly have been more different from one another. William A. Robertson had immigrated with his family to the United States in 1919, when he was eight. A dour Scot, silent and restless, he later described the festive Argilla Road life of my mother's family as the opposite of his own family experience. As soon as he could, he had fled Ipswich for the sea. When he met my mother, he was at loose ends, only recently returned from adventuring as a seaman on Byrd's second Antarctic expedition.

Their early years together were happy ones for my mother, she told me. When intimations of the coming World War reached Ipswich, they moved back into the summer cottage behind the barn and were employed at the nearby Robinson shipyard. Although most of the apple trees remained alive for many years afterward, my mother no longer dreamed that the orchard would survive. "When finally the farm came to an end," she later wrote, "and was no longer possible, it was the peaches that perished first, unloved and neglected. I came back in the spring to see them, and they were broken from the ice of a hard winter, their trunks rent and bleeding amber-colored tears. When I saw one last cluster of flowers on a dying tree, after all the years of disappointment and grief, I cried, too."

Early in 1938 nearly four acres, the peach orchard with its adjoining asparagus bed, were sold. Less than a year later, Kitty's mother deeded the remaining property to her youngest, most businesslike son. Her other son settled in California, while my parents and I stayed on as tenants.

The war sent my father, not yet an American citizen, off to the Merchant Marine Academy in 1940 and then on years of Lend-Lease and Murmansk runs. My mother hung on in Ipswich, managing to get an assembly-line job in the local Sylvania factory, where she became the union shop steward. We still lived on what had been the family farm, no longer her responsibility—no longer anything but memories.

For me, it was not an unhappy time, but for my mother it must have been very difficult. The cottage, built for summer use, was mostly uninsulated. Winter winds rushed in around the windows and through the walls; the pipes froze regularly. I well remember ice in the toilet and bathtub. It was so cold one wartime winter that even my mother gave up, probably for my sake, and we moved in for months with her mother in Boston.

The main house was empty during most of those years. We would walk by and peer through the windows at the darkened rooms. How I wondered at her stories of happy family gatherings. Once, we stood outside, both of us silent, while her brother ate alone by candlelight at the dining room table. In 1942 he sold more pieces of the land—a slice on the hillside to his brother, others to neighbors—proving that, as he had said years before, the land was best suited for houses, not apples.

The end of the war brought new beginnings. My father finished building a fishing boat, a dragger, which he had started in the barn before the war. In 1945, with savings from their wartime jobs, my mother bought from her brother the last remaining available piece of orchard land, a plot of almost four acres on the western side. There, in 1947–48, my parents built a small house a few feet from the marsh, siting it next to a vigorous young birch. Here she lived for the rest of her life.

Those years blur for me; I was involved with school and friends. My parents fished out of Annisquam on their dragger, *Kelpie,* leaving before dawn, returning in darkness when I was asleep. Later, my mother would write:

Exhausted from hours of backbreaking toil on the rolling deck of the *Kelpie,* in my uniform or smeared oilskins and scaly rubber boots, cutting fish in the keeler box while the seagulls screamed incessantly, I used to pause to think how lucky I was and how for once my sex had not prevented me from doing something that I had always wanted to do: work, really work on the sea; to be part, really part of the life of the sea.

Those four years on the *Kelpie,* the bitter winters and the broiling hot summers, were the high point of a long working life, and I thought my heart would break when I saw the *Kelpie* sailing away, sold, another hand on the wheel.

As with the orchard in earlier years, the *Kelpie* with her husband-and-wife team was too small to be economically viable. The strain of working so much together, after the war years of being so much apart, separated them again. After the sale of the boat, my father took a year-long job in the Arctic, helping to build Canadian–United States weather stations. "There is a kind of resilience acquired with the passing years," my mother once wrote. "The failures so often turn out to be only a shift of wind that sets the vessel sailing on a new course." She took advantage of this shift to travel back to the 1930s, writing this book and, by doing so, putting the farm behind her even as she brought it to life. It was as though by reliving those days she could say farewell without bitterness.

She intended to finish her book, I am sure. But after my father returned from the Arctic, there was no more quiet time. The simplest thing to say is that he returned with a nervous breakdown. The hardships of the farm years must have seemed tame compared with the difficulties of the fifteen years before his death, in 1968. In the orchard she could look ahead with a certain optimism: spring would come. There was nothing spring-like to look forward to with my father's illness. In addition there was the urgent need—yet again—to make a living. She got the first of a series of newspaper jobs, and the manuscript was put aside and then abandoned.

. . .

ALTHOUGH the orchard had been the focus of that manuscript, there had never been much talk at home about those years before I was alive, although I remember an undercurrent of sadness. For several autumns, my mother and I picked apples at the big Goodale Orchard, still thriving up the road—she all day on the ladders getting twenty-five to fifty cents a bushel, I after school on the ground picking up the bruised drops for cider, at fifteen cents. Good work, it seemed to me, but she hated it and swore she would never again eat an apple. Thinking back now, I don't recall her ever eating a single one.

To survive, I think, she had to move on without many backward glances. When the past was inescapable, as it must have been on the ladders of that orchard, or when we skirted her childhood home, she would talk of other things, never speaking of failure—never, I believe, thinking it. After all, the house and at least part of the land were still in the family. With a farmer's springtime exuberance and echoing her father's optimism of years before, she would say that tomorrow, this summer, next year . . . would surely be fine.

"In restless America, it is strange, I suppose, to be living still in the place where I was born: but here I am," she noted, close to the end of her seventy-eight years. Hers was, above all, a working life, and the working-class years never failed to inform her tireless later efforts as a radio reporter, local historian, town selectwoman, and "unofficial dean of Ipswich journalists," as one editorial put it after her death. Letters, articles, and obituaries mourned her below headlines that read: "Never retiring, never neutral, Kitty had guts"; "Kitty Robertson—an Ipswich legend"; and "Townspeople will miss the woman who cared." Minutes before that sudden and unexpected death in February 1979, she had delivered her weekly column to the *Ipswich Chronicle.* It was the orchard years that she had called back.

The first year was full of promise. Day after mild day made it happen so that after the end of the winter—the pruning done, the brush piled and burned, the trees fed—the burst of bloom in May, shell-pink blossoms against a sky of softest blue with drifts of puffy clouds, was splendid.

Then there was that terrible winter of 1933–34, that February when the thermometer hit twenty-four below zero and never once did the glass rise above ten degrees. Huddled on the sofa in the little circle of warmth from the Glenwood range, Freya, the Great Dane, and I spent day after day hibernating, while outside the snow blew incessantly past the kitchen window.

I never lost hope or doubted that from the Depression wreck I would be able to save the beloved place, this family center, cherished by my grandmother, my father, now by me, and who knew what generations to come.

And somehow we survived, Freya and I. When the first southwester brought the warm spring rain and downspouts and gutters drip drip dripped outside the window, I felt again the stirrings of hope and even a ghost of the old enthusiasm.

But never again in the four years that followed was there that sense of certainty of power, of inevitable victory. Grimly I struggled on, until in the end the Depression eased. My brother, who had been carrying on his own battle toward success, was able to step in and pluck the brands from the burning.

He was too wise and practical to bother with the apple trees, but it was they, after all, who saved the day just as my father said they would.

More than sixty years have passed since those hard days when the fruit of my mother's small orchard rescued the farm from the reaches of the bank. Now a new generation gathers in the old square farmhouse overlooking the salt marshes. But sometimes, walking home on a summer night, I hear a great horned owl calling from its nest in the ancient shagbark hickory on the hillside. At those moments I think I'm hearing what my mother must have heard, and I remember her story of the years before I was born, "that time of leveling," as she called it, "when we were all in the same boat," when she and her neighbors were kept afloat by the strength they found in one another.

—*Betsy Robertson Cramer*

ABOUT THE AUTHOR

ADELE CROCKETT ROBERTSON was born in 1901 at her family's farm in Ipswich, Massachusetts. After the orchard years, she was a writer with the WPA and worked in a shipyard and in a factory. At age fifty she became a journalist and won several New England Press Awards. A beloved local figure, Adele Crockett Robertson served as Ipswich selectwoman, and her commentary on current events and politics was widely read. The Ipswich Town Hall flew its flag at half-mast on the day she died in 1979.

BETSY ROBERTSON CRAMER, the author's daughter, contributed the foreword and epilogue to *The Orchard*. She lives presently in Santa Barbara, California.

ccc 12/05
Crat 2/06
OK 4/06
CPU10u
CG 2/07
OK 12/08
Crof 2/09
OK 9/12
TAP1/13
OK 10/14